How to Find Your Next Career

In a Job Market That Expects You to Fit In

SNOWFLAKES, ZEBRAS, *and* FINGERPRINTS

By
Maryann Lombardi

Snowflakes, Zebras, and Fingerprints:
How to Find Your Next Career Move and Stand Out in a Job Market That Expects You to Fit In

MARYANN LOMBARDI

Copyright © 2024 - Reflek Publishing

All Rights Reserved.

No part of this publication may be reproduced, distributed, or transmitted in any form or by any means, including photocopying, recording, or other electronic or mechanical methods, without the prior written permission of the publisher, except in the case of brief quotations embodied in critical reviews and certain other noncommercial uses permitted by copyright law.

Disclaimer: The author makes no guarantees concerning the level of success you may experience by following the advice and strategies contained in this book, and you accept the risk that results will differ for each individual. The purpose of this book is to educate, entertain, and inspire.

For more information: maryann@maryannlombardi.com

ISBN (paperback): 978-1-962280-29-7
ISBN (ebook): 978-1-962280-28-0

Dedication

To Mike Gargano,
whose one introduction changed
the course of my life.

To my parents, John and Cathryn,
who never fail to be there when I need them.
Their faith in me has moved mountains,
and they've always been supportive as fuck.
(Sorry Mom, for using the f-word.)

Table of Contents

Author's Note 7

Part One 11
1. Divorce Was the Best Thing to Happen to Me 13
2. Choose Your Own Adventure 19
3. The Right Fit 27
4. Lonely as Fuck 33
5. One Introduction Changed My Life 45
6. Networking Is Like Sex 51
7. Résumés Are a Crappy Way of Measuring Your Skills ... 61
8. Blame the System, Not Yourself 69
9. Fifteen Thousand Feet to Freedom 79
10. I Can See the Top of the Washington
Monument from My Classroom 89
11. Mom, You're Kinda Low-Key Thriving 97

Part Two 107
Section One: Career Change Kick-Start 113
12. What Do You Want? 115

13. The Right-Fit Matrix 129
14. Your Career Growth Strategy 141
15. The Hidden Job Market 157

Section Two: Mastering Your Business Relationships 167
16. Who's in Your Circle? 169
17. Building and Nurturing Your Relationships 179
18. What to Say When Networking 193
19. Self-Promotion and Your Career Story 205

Section Three: Career Momentum—What Gets in Your Way 215
20. The Introvert/Extrovert Narrative 217
21. Time Management 225
22. Negative Self-Talk 233
23. How Do You Know You're Making Progress? 239

Here's What to Do Next 245
Acknowledgments 247
Make a Lasting Impact in Real Time 249
About the Author 251

Author's Note

Dear Friends and Strangers,

Hi! Thank you for picking up the book and jumping into this journey with me. Right now we find ourselves together, the moment before we begin. It feels surprising not to see your face or hear your voice, as I felt oddly in conversation with you while writing this. Is it possible we already know each other? Or is that presumptuous? Maybe. But it is also most likely true.

So many of our experiences are shared, even when they are individual to our own unique identities, circumstances, and feelings. Like snowflakes, zebras, and fingerprints, no matter how much our shapes, stripes, and ridges resemble each other, our lived experience is painfully and beautifully unique to each and every one of us.

This is a book about work, but is anything really about just one thing? Our work lives are inextricably linked to everything else. Our career provides the currency that facilitates the life we live.

At times our work defines us, chaperones us as we make lifelong friends, and provides a structure for our growth. It can also confine, smother, and—like a charismatic cult leader—govern us into submission.

This book is also about power, people, and perspective. It's about the *power* you have to change your mind, discover and do what you want, and live a life that matters to you while your career does its job to support you in that effort. It's about the significance of your relationships with *people* and how they reshape your beliefs about yourself and the opportunities that surround you. And finally, it includes the practical tools you'll need to flip the *perspective* on how to navigate a career change, get the job you want, and build your confidence.

The book is separated into two parts. The first, a memoir: eleven essays that explore my personal journey through divorce and family court; single-parenting; a career exploration that started in New York City cabaret clubs and led to helping thousands of people get jobs, access mental health support, and build their businesses; and how one introduction changed the course of my life. The second, a guide for finding your next right-fit career move with clear, tactical advice and action steps using a proven framework that has not only helped me navigate my own career opportunities but has also supported hundreds of individuals to grow in their work.

The first section will provide context for the second. It's difficult to do the *what* when you don't understand the *why*, so start at the beginning if you can, and let's share the ride. See you in there.

With love,
Maryann

Don't spend time beating on a wall, hoping it will transform into a door.
—*Coco Chanel*

Part One

1

DIVORCE WAS THE BEST THING TO HAPPEN TO ME

Once upon a time, there was a girl who lived in a castle. The castle was in a museum. When the children came to the museum, they pressed as close as they could to the glass globe in which the castle quietly sat. For they had heard if they looked hard enough, they could see the girl who lived inside, the girl in the castle inside the museum.

—KATE BERNHEIMER

I went into labor six and a half weeks early. After a trip to our community hospital, an unsuccessful attempt to stop my labor, and a profanity-filled ambulance ride down to the teaching hospital, which had a NICU, I popped out the little love of my life. My child was perfect.

Snowflakes, Zebras, *and* Fingerprints

Words have always fascinated me.

A word like "perfect" conjures some idealized vision of whatever it attaches to and describes. According to our common understanding, something that is perfect is without defect or blemish. Let's be honest here: my child came into this world with some defects. Underdeveloped lungs, for example. A yellow tint caused by an immature liver, along with a full blood transfusion to stave off some terrible thing that no one explained to me at the time. Their little body was a bundle of contradictions. They were big even with their shortened time in the oven, and their impatience to escape the confines of my body was followed by an extended stay in an incubator, tacked down with tubes and pumps.

But they were still perfect to me. It is a powerful feeling to know you can see something that—in the eyes of doctors, in-laws, and other people—is underdeveloped, immature, and inadequate.

Months before, my husband and I had moved to western Massachusetts after a decade in New York City. We wanted to be closer to my parents, and I was set to start graduate school in a couple of months. In hindsight, it seems absurd that I thought I could begin my master's program when I was due to have a baby. But never being one to plan my life in that much detail, it hadn't occurred to me it would be a challenge.

Like parenting, financial literacy, and divorce, no one teaches you how to do it; you have to figure it out as you go. Certainly, many

1

people want to give you parenting advice, to tell you what *they* did or how *they* survived after the fact, which feels more like catharsis for them than education for you. There is a reason no one teaches you how to go through a divorce, because if you knew all the shit that would go down, why the fuck would you willingly choose to put yourself (and the other person) through that? Regarding financial literacy, there is no excuse for it not being more of a priority, but that is a conversation for another day.

* * *

My divorce was one of the best things to happen to me. That sounds weird to say, but it is undoubtedly true. Breaking my world apart provided the necessary opportunity to rebuild it.

When my child was three, I remember sitting in the grass, watching them play and discussing something unbelievable they had just discovered. They giggled at how the grass tickled their hands and got frustrated when they couldn't keep count of the clouds passing by. They mumbled, yanked weeds from the ground, and I watched as if a whole world of activity was bursting like fireworks inside their mind. Stories evolved, and characters emerged as flowers danced with blades of grass and dandelion puffballs exploded in front of me.

I sat there listening, observing, curious about what was happening behind the little door that protected their imagination. Did it look like the magical realism that danced off the page in *The Girl in the Castle Inside the Museum*, one of my child's favorite picture books? Maybe it was like *Santa's Toy Shop*, with elves running around in chaos a few days before Christmas, building stuff and then packing it away. Or the M.C. Escher painting with staircases that seem to go nowhere and everywhere simultaneously. While I sat there, two thoughts interrupted my wondering:

1. *I can't remember the last time I felt this much joy.*
2. *I feel like a shitty mom, and I don't want to feel this way anymore.*

I was numb and exhausted from the challenges in my marriage. Plus, the workload in grad school, teaching, and trying to keep my kid from running into traffic took all my energy, making it almost impossible to be present with my child. I know you know that feeling. It would be hard to find a mom or a woman who hasn't felt that way at some point. The overwhelm. The fatigue. The disappointment in yourself for not being better. The burden of having to hold it all together, to be everything for everyone but nothing for yourself, and the feeling of failure if you acknowledge or even speak your struggle out loud.

"Fuck," I said to myself. "This isn't sustainable."

I made a decision that day in the grass: I wanted more of that joy; I was desperate for it.

Over the next couple of days, weeks, or months—it's hard to recover the timeframe—I let my mind wander. What would

1

that joyful life look like? What would it feel like? I couldn't see it clearly, but flashes of images and feelings would push against me like a flood of water trying to break down a door jammed too tightly. I could hear a soundtrack tuning in the distance and feel time ticking, allowing myself to sink into what it would be like to feel truly loved by a partner. To see in their eyes, hear in their voice, and feel in their body love for me, not the anger or indifference I usually experienced.

After imagining that life, coming back to reality just didn't fit. Like I was in the wrong place, at the wrong time, in the wrong body, wearing something that didn't make sense on my frame anymore. It didn't stretch as I moved. It confined me in all the places I needed it to breathe. The fabric itched and scratched where I wanted something smooth or soft. I had trimmed, tucked, and done my best at modifications, but in the end, all the alterations left me uncovered and cold.

* * *

Some moments in our lives provide an unobstructed view of what we need to see, of what is possible. But we have to stop long enough to let it come into focus. With all the noise, momentum, distractions, expectations, responsibilities, and pressures, it can feel impossible to pull the hand brake. Those moments that change our perspective are often quiet; at least, they have been for me. That day in the grass, no beam of light showed me the way. I didn't get hit over the head metaphorically with the answer to my problems, just a clear, quiet fork in the road.

I could continue the path I was on and lose myself further—or I could change.

2

CHOOSE YOUR OWN ADVENTURE

Life is either a daring adventure or nothing at all.

—HELEN KELLER

Start where you are. Use what you have. Do what you can.

—ARTHUR ASHE

My kid is an emotional, artsy, nerdy, introvert with wild and curly hair, a goofy sense of style, and big heart. They are much smarter than I am, with better boundaries and a sense of themselves that probably developed in utero. They also love games: video games, role-playing games, card games, traditional board games—all of it.

Whenever they are home from college, we make pizza and continue our Super Sorry! tournament/dance party. Game play is simple: we have combined two Sorry! games on one board, and we draw and move until our playlist demands a dance break. The game Sorry! became popular in the US in the 1950s and—like Monopoly, Scrabble, Candy Land, and Trouble (who didn't love that little pop-o-matic inverted dice bowl)—has been a staple of the classic board-game canon ever since.

I enjoy games as much as your average person. My card-playing skills are up to par thanks to my mom, and I like board games thanks to my '80s childhood, but video games have never captivated me. The most time I have spent playing a video game happened in the back of the Asheville Pinball Museum in North Carolina one weekend, a couple summers ago. In a dark, nondescript room behind a maze of pinball machines from every decade sat multiple beeping and flashing classic arcade games. In the corner stood *Frogger*. Without the prying eyes of, well, anyone, I dedicated myself to that little green frog, helping him reach his destination without splatting on the pixelated pavement.

My kid can spend hours lost in a video game world, discovering twists and turns, rolling their eyes at cheesy backstories, and riding the roller coaster of adrenaline that peaks as they try yet again to beat the big boss.

Upon request, sometimes I'll sit next to them and watch them play. As the player, you follow a quest. You have limited access to new paths, lifelines, potions, and treasure, until you unlock them by solving a puzzle or overcoming a challenge. The games are an intricate web of possibilities, fun, and adventure, depending on your commitment and effort to unlock the opportunities. You don't know what you will find, what you will face, or who you will encounter, but you have enough faith (and experience) to know it will be worth finding out—so you play.

When exploring why people loves games, *New York Times* game maker Sam Von Ehren wrote, "The game designer Sid Meier once remarked that 'a game is a series of interesting choices.' Navigating these choices shapes the course of play, revealing who we are and how we think. Playing a game is an act of exposition."[1] As we explore the game play, our actions betray our beliefs and motivations; they illustrate more about how we think and what we want than even our words can.

Those video game worlds my kid loves are like the *Choose Your Own Adventure* books of my childhood. The *Choose* books were created by two single dads, with the insight and expertise of their kids. The series recognized that our narratives are not confined by one storyline. They are a web of plotlines you can choose that interweave, branch off, and build into a rich adventure.

According to a *New Yorker* article, one of the author's daughters, Andrea, described the books as "a way of encouraging kids to experience the world through exploration and curiosity." She looked at her father's diagrams that mapped the storylines as

---

1. Sam Von Ehren, "Why Do People Love Games?," *New York Times*, updated June 12, 2020, https://www.nytimes.com/2020/06/11/style/why-people-love-games.html.

"forking branches spidering across taped-together paper charts. To her, "those charts felt like houses of possibility."[2]

Isn't that what our life should be? Houses of possibility?

We are not locked to one story. Just because the original storyline sent us in one direction, that doesn't mean it needs to continue down the same path. We can choose to change it. We are changing all the time when we are young, bouncing from one reality to the next. Trying things on, playing at being anything we can imagine. Why does that adventure have to end? Why do we stop imagining that a unicorn could be best friends with a cloud and they could travel the neighborhood, fighting crime and eating ice cream? When do we stop trusting that our dreams can become our reality?

When do we stop choosing our own adventure?

* * *

I wasn't much of a dreamer as a child. Dreaming wasn't encouraged the way *doing* was. It was actually a pretty cool way to grow up. Nothing was off limits. If I wanted to accomplish something, my parents were supportive as long as I was committed and took action (and it obeyed the laws of physics and was legal).

---

2. Leslie Jamison, "The Enduring Allure of Choose Your Own Adventure Books," *New Yorker*, September 12, 2022, https://www.newyorker.com/magazine/2022/09/19/the-enduring-allure-of-choose-your-own-adventure-books.

2

My artsy and entrepreneurial spirit catapulted me into creative disciplines in my youth and in both my undergrad and graduate degrees. And to their credit, my parents never pushed me to do something more practical, or to choose a career or activity that might make more money. If I did the work, they did whatever they could to support me. It has always been a real gift.

My creativity, can-do spirit, and the confidence and independence nurtured by my parents fired my productivity. Whatever my ideas, I quickly turn them into action. I can always see a path to getting something done. It keeps me building and launching businesses, programs, or partnerships, finding creative ways to problem-solve, and bringing people together to make it all happen. But my doing-over-dreaming philosophy has also made me resistant to stopping my momentum long enough to indulge my imagination.

Playing in the dreamworld scares me in an odd way. It grabs ahold of an insecurity and vulnerability I don't fully understand, especially if I can't immediately see how to turn the dream into reality.

I didn't know how to achieve the joy I was seeking. Creating a new life seemed daunting and a little absurd. My entire life was wrapped up in this relationship, this marriage. How doesn't anyone entangle that?

* * *

The work to change our lives, personally or professionally, requires us to look *inside* ourselves for guidance and search *outside* ourselves for support. It is an ebb and flow between these two things. If we don't do the inner work, it is hard to be strategic about the support we need from others. If we only do the inner work but never reach out for support, we lose all momentum and get stuck in our head. They are symbiotic.

Sometimes what we want is clear; other times it is shrouded in fear and responsibility. Maybe you are just trying to get through the day, leave a toxic workplace, or keep from screaming at the top of your lungs for everyone to move out of your effing way. Maybe you just need room to breathe so you can think and figure it out. Maybe you are avoiding thinking about it because of the flood that will occur if you actually allow yourself to get into it.

Creating time to breathe and knowing what matters to you is crucial because it filters out all of the stuff that gets in the way of your progress. It narrows your focus so you can take action to achieve your personal or professional goals with more efficiency and clarity. It also reduces the stress of indecision. But guess what: knowing what you *don't* want does the same thing.

Staring down a divorce and what I didn't know at the time would turn into an arduous journey toward that new life. I found myself overwhelmed trying to clarify what I wanted. When I couldn't, I focused on what I didn't want. The interplay of those two things helped me start taking action toward that new life.

2

I knew I wanted

- more of the joy I felt in the grass with my child;
- more adventure with my child and in my day-to-day life, even though I didn't know what adventure really meant at the time; and
- a job I enjoyed that would take advantage of my unique skills—something that would offer me a fresh start and allow me to get out of Massachusetts and move somewhere with more opportunity.

I didn't want to

- feel numb or live in a house underscored by low-grade anger all the time;
- feel like a terrible parent; and
- continue working for crap money or take a job I really didn't want just to get through this transition.

3

THE RIGHT FIT

Let's start with the obvious…if it won't zip, snap, or close without you going through contortions, it's too small. If you can't reach, lift your arms or bend over without things binding, they don't fit you properly.

—JENNIFER CONNOLLY

Change is painful, but nothing is as painful as staying stuck somewhere you don't belong.

—MANDY HALE

During a conversation with my first divorce lawyer, she said something that has always stuck with me. After explaining all the reasons why I wanted to leave my marriage, I said, "But it's not like he cheated or was physically abusive or anything."

"He doesn't have to be," she said, cutting me off. "You don't need a justification to go through this process," she continued. "I know that *you* need to know why, and that is important for you, but you don't have to explain yourself to me or to anyone. Whatever the reason is, you have the right and the opportunity to make a change and get out. Don't let anyone tell you differently."

Somewhere deep down, I believed the only defensible reasons to leave my marriage, to quit, were infidelity or physical abuse. Because if it wasn't for those, why would I ever leave, and how would I explain it? Was my mental health and happiness actually a worthy reason to disassemble my life, his life, and our child's?

I have been in way too many conversations with other women, friends, and colleagues who, when contemplating leaving their relationship, have felt the same way. "It would just be easier if he hit me or something," they say. There is nothing easier about being in or leaving a physically abusive relationship. Yet by staying, we subjugate our happiness, autonomy, and dreams. We think that to want something different—to need something more—we need an irrefutable reason that everyone will understand.

We are so used to changing ourselves to fit into things that aren't right, assuming we are the problem. Whether it's fashion, relationships, or jobs, we squeeze, starve, and contort ourselves to try and make it work instead of acknowledging that sometimes it's not the right fit and it's time to move on. And we hope our

3

effort is noticed, appreciated, and rewarded with a kind word, an offer of support, or a promotion. Sometimes it is, but for many of us, it isn't, which leads to more frustration, burnout, stress, and disillusionment about what to do next.

It is tricky to determine or admit when the fit is off. We are so used to making it work, no matter the fit, that we gloss over the itch and accept the piping poking us in the back. We go ahead and buy yet another dress without pockets, no matter how desperate we are for one with, because that is what we are offered, and we are used to sacrificing our comfort. We deal with it.

* * *

After that day in the grass, I was suddenly aware of my performance, trying to fit into my life. I was in the habit of doing anything I could to keep the peace, stay on safe topics, go to bed early, or stay up late—anything to get by. It had seemed normal to behave that way, but now it just felt dishonest. Trying to reassemble what had begun to erode too many years ago seemed impossible. I'd had a panic attack after a couple of sessions with the first marriage counselor we talked to, years before this point. In that room, my husband felt free to tell me everything that was "wrong" with me. I didn't have the skills to communicate my own feelings in response, nor did I feel safe in that room to figure it out. The next counselor we spoke to said simply, "If you aren't here to fix your marriage, if you have already decided you are done, there is not much I can do for you."

Once I had seen a glimpse of what my life could look like, once I had tasted it with all my senses and let my mind linger on the possibility of a new reality, I couldn't unsee it. It's like when you're twelve and you catch your parents having sex. You can't unsee that, no matter how hard you try. Thankfully, that never happened to me, but I can imagine how burned into your brain it would be!

As writer Sophia Benoit explained in an article for *GQ*, "*Crazy. Psycho. Bitch.* All of those things get thrown at women—sometimes all at the same time. Most women have, at one time or another, been slapped with those labels just for voicing totally normal and healthy concerns and boundaries." Benoit went on to say that women are "constantly told that we're overreacting," and that as a woman, "you get good at shrinking down your emotional needs and expectations, just to make sure you don't come across as 'crazy.'"[3]

Whether we're trained to be seen and not heard or told to get along and be grateful for what we have, images and language bombard us, reinforcing that we are not enough. When we have managed to deal with all that, we step into a dressing room, try on a pair of pants in our size that won't even make it over our hips, and shame ourselves for what is a flaw in fashion, not a defect in ourselves.

It is standard operating procedure to adjust ourselves, our needs, and our way of moving through the world to fit everything else

---

3. Sophia Benoit, "Why Women Say Nothing Is Wrong When Something Is Clearly Wrong," *GQ*, June 20, 2018, https://www.gq.com/story/everything-is-fine.

around us. Whether in our personal or professional lives, our survival depends on it. It's almost unnoticeable, but once you notice it, it's hard to unsee it. As researcher and author Caroline Criado Perez states in her book *Invisible Women*, "The truth is that around the world, women continue to be disadvantaged by a working culture that is based on the ideological belief that male needs are universal."[4]

It is safer for a man to drive or ride in a car, as the safety features that crash test dummies help refine are mostly designed around the size of a standard man. Office temperatures are scientifically set to the comfort level of men, which makes them three to five degrees too cold for women. Even the open office plan makes many women feel uncomfortable, says Professor Pragya Agarwal, international speaker and consultant on inclusive workplaces, and visiting professor at the University of Oxford:

> Research and surveys have shown that open plan offices make women feel vulnerable, and are an ambient, subtle form of sexism. Women report as "always being watched," a covert form of bullying, thereby aggravating anxiety. These kind of office layouts can reinforce power dynamics already at play in a work environment.[5]

---

4. Caroline Criado Perez, *Invisible Women: Data Bias in a World Designed for Men* (New York: Harry N. Abrams, 2021).

5. Pragya Agarwal, "It's Time We Address the Male Bias in Workplace Design," *LinkedIn Pulse*, November 12, 2018, https://www.linkedin.com/pulse/its-time-we-address-male-bias-workplace-design-dr-pragya-agarwal/.

Women are certainly not the only marginalized group layered with expectations or who have to find a way to fit into a world not designed for them. Yet living up to the roles of ambitious leader, compassionate caregiver, damn good cook, sexy partner, attentive friend, and health and fitness phenom presses down on us like one of those weighted blankets that are supposed to be comfortable but feel claustrophobic instead. All this to say, it is not only challenging to notice when the fit is off; it's counterintuitive to act on it. But we must take action. Without it, we find ourselves stuck shrinking to match everything else around us instead of expanding to meet the size of our dreams.

Like that *Choose Your Own Adventure* story, we get to decide what path we go down, then change our mind and try another. We can stop forcing ourselves through a career, a job, or a life that feels uncomfortable, undesirable, devaluing, unchallenging, and too confined. Just as that lawyer told me, you don't need to defend it to others. You only need to understand why you think it's time to choose a new adventure, and then take action to make it so.

Change is hard, but so what? Do the hard thing. You can handle it. You can survive it. You will thrive because of it. And the truth is, shoving yourself into a box, jeans, a marriage, or a career that no longer fits is hard too. Which challenge would you rather embrace?

4

LONELY AS FUCK

I used to think the worse thing in life was to end up alone. It's not. The worst thing in life is to end up with people that make you feel alone.

—ROBIN WILLIAMS

We are lonely as fuck.

Blame it on technology, long work days sandwiched between commutes, the decline of civic engagement, our migration away from living intergenerationally, or the independent spirit of the American ethos run amok. According to a consumer study around technology from the summer of 2023, a third of

Americans say they "feel lonelier now, more than ever before."[6] And healthcare company Cigna recently commissioned data showing that 58 percent of Americans *always* feel lonely.[7]

That's terrible.

We are in a connection-rich and relationship-poor time. How is it possible we are connected to more people than at any other time in history, yet still lonely as fuck? Our connections and the technology that fosters them keep us in a dopamine loop that makes us feel worse in the long run, even as we get hit with a momentary high from all the likes, DMs, and texts. Our relationships and the time it takes to develop and nurture them suffer as social media scrolling, caregiving responsibilities, overwork, and the status we seem to get from being busy take priority.

Life events like divorce, job loss, a death in the family, or the birth of a baby reshape our understanding of ourselves and the composition of our support system. And a dependence on technology to drive our social relationships contributes profoundly to our deep loneliness. So do mental, physical, and emotional exhaustion, and workplace burnout.

---

6. Alexa Mikhail, "We are '50% human and 50% technology,' and it's fueling an American health crisis," *Fortune WELL*, August 11, 2023, https://fortune.com/well/2023/08/11/loneliness-study-digital-social-media/.

7. Sophie Okolo, "Why Americans Are Lonely and What We Can Do About It," *Forbes*, February 24, 2023, https://www.forbes.com/sites/sophieokolo/2023/02/24/why-americans-are-lonely-and-what-we-can-do-about-it/?sh=613492c32dbf.

American journalist and author Anne Helen Petersen has been writing about what she calls the Friendship Dip. She describes how our friendships wax and wane as we age, due to shifting priorities around family and work:

> The biggest problem, of course, is work—and not just normal work, but all-consuming work, slippery work, work that becomes the central axis of our lives, either out of necessity or compulsion. But the secondary problem is American individualism, which compels bourgeois Americans to focus what small amount of energy we have either on optimizing ourselves (exercise, skin care, "self-care") or on our very close familial circle (that amorphous, ever-expanding activity known as "parenting" that includes everything from making Spirit Week costumes to kids' sports).[8]

* * *

When my child was four, we moved out of the house we shared with their dad and into the unfinished home my parents were building less than ten miles away. Aspirational in size, the house loomed over our little twosome. My mother designed it to hold the whole family for a couple of moments a year when we would all arrive. Absent those family gatherings, it was cavernous. We mostly lived upstairs, which housed three guest bedrooms and

---

8. Anne Helen Petersen, "The Friendship Dip," *Culture Study* (blog/newsletter), November 5, 2023, https://annehelen.substack.com/p/the-friendship-dip.

a bathroom, all connected by a central landing with a staircase descending toward the front door.

I have loved being a single parent. Too many conversations on single-parenting focus on the challenges instead of the opportunities. Now, let's be real: there are some challenges in single-parenting, especially for those without the social or financial safety net that can provide them with things like an unfinished house to live in. But there are opportunities as well. The role our uninterrupted one-on-one time together played in building the closeness my child and I share cannot be understated.

Those first couple of years in that house are some of my favorite memories—just the two of us, one-on-one, without distraction. So many of the rituals, patterns, and the ethos that came to define our new life began upstairs in that house. We played games and had epic craft battles; their picture books transformed into operettas; spiders made out of foam balls climbed the banister to our haven; paper pom-poms hung from the ceiling; and a curtain made from four layers of ribbon marked the entrance to their room. It was a beautiful madness upstairs!

There still exists this idea that the nuclear family, which includes two people who are married to each other—one cisgender man and one cisgender woman—is the right way to raise children. It may be the right way for some.

4

By the way, did you ever play that adolescent fortune-cookie game as a preteen? The one where you would add "in bed" to the end of your fortune? After snapping the cookie apart, you'd slide out a fortune that read, "An exciting opportunity lies ahead of you," and the fortune would become, "An exciting opportunity lies ahead of you, in bed." Please tell me my friends and I weren't the only ones who played that game.

Carrying on the tradition, I think it's time to start adding "for some" at the end of most of our declarations about how people should live their lives. "The hetero/cisgender two-parent family is the best way to raise a kid" would turn into "The hetero/cisgender two-parent family is the best way to raise a kid, for some." Or "Two parents staying together is best for the kids—for some."

* * *

My child was a headstrong, vibrant, emotional, and creative four-year-old, characteristics that follow them to this day. At the time, they had trouble staying in their room at night and vehemently rejected having their door closed. They would scream if they woke up and the door wasn't wide-open after falling asleep during story time, and they would run, panicked, into my room and climb into bed to sleep with me. I had assumed their anxiety was due to their age or the stress of navigating a new routine, but years later, they corrected my memory.

"Monsters hung out on the landing at night," they explained.

"What? Are you kidding me?" I asked.

"Nope. At night they would appear, and I was scared they would come into my room." They explained that the only place they felt safe from those freeloading beasts was in my room.

"Why didn't you tell me?"

"I don't know," they said.

When my brother was about the same age, he had trouble sleeping because of the dragons that populated the backyard. Our father went out one night and slayed them all as my brother directed him where to slash and swing his imaginary sword. When it was over, he never saw the dragons again.

Had I known, I may have skipped the blade, opting to invite the monsters for a cocktail to see if we could collaborate on a resolution that didn't involve them hanging outside my kid's room and scaring the shit out of them. Instead, to solve what I thought was a "closing the door" problem, I created a curtain. I pinned layers of ribbon across the top of the doorframe, and the curtain cascaded softly to the floor. It created an enchanted, protective gate from the landing and ushered my child into their little oasis.

4

They loved it.

I loved it.

Something about that ribbon curtain helped them feel more comfortable in their room and safe at night. They would stand in the doorframe, swaddled by the ribbon, and smile ear to ear. I could hear them playing, the bits and pieces of stories developing, and the worlds they created on the other side of the curtain.

Watching them run back and forth through that curtain made me think about my journey. On one side, I was dealing with my own kind of monsters and desperately trying to get to the other side. Divorce proceedings were in full swing. Mediation had failed, lawyers were engaged, custody was contentious, and the pressure was mounting. In the light, I felt a bit stronger; I could see the creatures, put on my armor for a battle, or hold my ground if a standoff occurred. But in the dark, it was terrifying; those beasts seemed to pound on the door, yelling and screaming. I never knew when they would break it down, squashing my dreams underneath the debris.

When I was alone in the house, sometimes I would walk back and forth through that ribbon curtain and stand in the middle of the doorframe myself, to feel an ounce of the whimsy and peace my kid felt in the same spot. Afterward, I would sit on their bed and wonder if the ribbon curtain could keep the monsters away from me too. Their room was comfortable and soft, with rounded edges and stuffed animals perched all around as if to ask, "Can I give you a hug?" *I get it*, I thought. *There are no monsters that can get me on this side of the curtain—and yes, you can absolutely give me a hug.*

* * *

During this time, I was lonely as fuck.

I got through it, thanks to support that came from expected and unexpected places. My parents were terrific. One of our family friends became a confidant and, when I started commuting to DC, would come over at four in the morning to get my child up, fed, and on the school bus so I could make my flight. I met other parents through my kid's school who had their own marital or relationship journeys. We bonded and created an informal circle of mutual support. Out of all my pre-divorce friends, only one of them kept in touch with me regularly. She lived thousands of miles away but called and sent cards. I have a magnet she sent me during that time with a sun on it, which still lives in my car almost fifteen years later.

Whether working through a divorce, navigating the ups and downs of a life well lived, or finding a new job, it is easier to make it through with people in your corner. Looking back, many people stood out as pivotal to my personal and professional growth. Some protected my sanity and made me feel loved, supported, and cared for. Others let me know, directly and indirectly, that what I wanted and needed was important. Some I was close to; others were strangers, peers, or colleagues. You never know who will say what you need to hear the most on any given day, make the burden you carry more manageable just because they can, or smile in a way that communicates, "You matter."

Our relationships are the key driver toward feeling less lonely. Those relationships help us feel connected to ourselves and each other, provide a sense of belonging, and help us grow in ways we may or may not expect. A good relationship allows you to be yourself; it includes trust, respect, open and honest conversation, and it is reciprocal.

We have thousands of followers, connections, and friends throughout social media, but that doesn't make us feel any more connected. Technology lulls us into thinking that convenience and access to more people equals more connectedness. But likes, texts, and DMs won't replace the power of spending time with someone—that exchange of energy, interest, and care.

Social media deceives us into thinking that more is better. The more people we are connected to, the more belonging we will feel. The more extensive our network, the more opportunities will flow to us. The more money we have, the better life we will have. The more I work, the more I will be valued and promoted. The more-is-better philosophy is a gluttonous cycle that leaves us feeling burned out and lonelier in our work and life. Consider what Michael Easter wrote in his bestselling book *The Comfort Crisis*.

> Scientists at Brigham Young University found that it doesn't matter how old you are or how much money you have, being lonely increases your risk of dying in the next 7 years by 26 percent. Overall, it can shorten life by 15 years. That's equivalent to smoking half a pack of cigarettes a day. Good relationships are also, according to another study conducted over 80 years by researchers at Harvard, a key ingredient to happiness across your lifespan. Good relationships beat fortune and fame.[9]

If the people you know are your lifeline to opportunity and your path to happiness and longevity, then reconnecting with and nurturing those relationships needs to be a priority. All of this is interconnected. Nothing happens in a vacuum. Just like your knee bone is connected to your thigh bone, which is connected to your hip bone, your happiness is connected to your fulfillment; your fulfillment is connected to your personal and professional opportunities, your opportunities are connected to your relationships, and on and on.

When we start something new, we are often overwhelmed by everything we have left behind, and obsessed with everything

---

9. Michael Easter, *The Comfort Crisis: Embrace Discomfort to Reclaim Your Wild, Happy, Healthy Self* (Emmaus, PA: Rodale Books, 2021).

we will gain. We can lose sight of what's in the middle—the things and the people who will help us get from where we are to where we want to be. Our vision, that dream of whatever is on the other side of where we are now, fuels our change. The community surrounding us is the support we need to put that accelerant into drive. A bit of that community might be standing beside us, ready to help.

Most of it, though, will be waiting in the wings.

5

ONE INTRODUCTION CHANGED MY LIFE

A couple of words is all it'll take to make everything in my life Before and After.

—KAREN M. MCMANUS

Back in 2010, I bought a row house in Washington, DC. At the time, I lived in western Massachusetts with a four-year-old, and a contentious custody battle was in full swing. I'm all for retail therapy, but I didn't even have permission to live outside the state with my child, so dropping cash on real estate in DC was financially irresponsible and a cry for help.

Desperate to start a new life after divorce, I felt panicked about my lack of control, and pissed that my fate was in the hands of some judge who didn't know me. While sitting in family court, he made it clear that he wouldn't permit me to leave the state of Massachusetts without a job in the place I wanted to move to. In hindsight, that seems pretty reasonable; I found it infuriating at the time.

I knew I would find a job. I have always had a knack for finding or creating work opportunities through the businesses I've built or working with governments or institutions to create a job for me. But the judge didn't give a shit about what I knew I could do; he didn't care about my résumé, my hard or soft skills, or my confidence. He wouldn't take my word for it. He needed an offer letter, proof someone had hired me.

After I explored moving to North Carolina or Colorado, I fell in love with Washington, DC. Years earlier, while still married, my ex-husband and I had talked about moving there to be closer to my brother and cousin, who were also working their way to the area. Plus, DC is amazing; it is so much more than the chaos the news makes it out to be, full of community, culture, and opportunity—and damn, did I need all of that.

The opportunity was the most pressing since I could barely support myself and my family from the directorship job I had at the time. I was building partnerships and programs between the University of Massachusetts Amherst, the government of the City of Springfield, media organizations, and the community to create jobs and bring attention to the region. I loved the work but the pay wasn't sustainable.

I needed a job that indicated responsibility and security. But I didn't want any old job; I wanted a good one that fit my skills and interests, something that was challenging and allowed me to pay my bills. I wanted a job that was the right fit.

Too often, in moments of desperation, we take any opportunity (or any relationship, for that matter) instead of the right opportunity (or right relationship). But what was the point of going through all of this stuff—divorce, family court, changing my life—if I wasn't going to build a life that brought joy, love, and adventure? A life that left fear, anger, and isolation in the past.

I had been traveling back and forth from MA to DC, learning about the city and its challenges, looking for career opportunities in the gaps, places and problems that my skills and experience were uniquely suited to solve. So much opportunity exists in the space between the current staff's roles and responsibilities, and the work that needs to get done. As organizations are growing, adapting, or even tightening, leaders often need people to help them accelerate through the transition in ways the existing roles and responsibilities aren't equipped to do. They may need someone to solve acute problems, build new programs or partnerships, upgrade business operations, or create ways for divisions to collaborate more effectively.

With my eclectic set of skills and a work history that didn't fit neatly into most job descriptions, simply applying for jobs clearly wasn't getting me the kind of career opportunity I wanted. I knew there was work—there is always work to be done—but finding it was the challenge. Similar to what it is like when you are raising money, it is rarely an issue of whether there is enough of it. There is always money, and there are always jobs; the obstacle is getting access. Access is the issue, and it is granted through your relationships.

I needed to get in front of the right people to pitch myself, but I couldn't figure out how. After endless coffee dates, happy hours, lunches, and months of trying it alone, I called Mike.

Have you ever walked that thin line, balancing heartache, panic, and probably some undiagnosed depression? Holding it together for the people around you, but screaming "WTF!" on repeat in your mind? That was my state of mind when I jumped on a call with Mike. So when he said, "How can I help you?" I nearly cried.

Mike is one of the most well-networked people I know. He is a family friend who worked for my dad for years. That professional relationship grew into a personal one, which led Mike to become an essential member of our family's inner circle. He is wiry and strong, with a runner's frame and a sharp focus that makes you feel equally a little nervous and completely safe at the same time. When I asked him years later what role relationships have played for him in his life and career, he said, "It's been about 100 percent. Yeah. I mean, honestly, 100 percent."

5

My father knows many people but is unapologetic at his advanced age of not needing many friends. Throughout his life, he has had strong friendships; many of his friends have subsequently died, some who he thought were his friends betrayed that trust, and others have faded in and out. Such is the path of life, I imagine him thinking, but it weighs on him deeper down.

On the other hand, my mother can make friends with everyone she comes in contact with. It's hard not to like her, and if you're not careful, you will find yourself telling her all your innermost secrets, which she will probably relay to everyone else. Sitting in the row ahead of me on a flight during my teenage years, she chatted with the gentleman seated next to her from the moment we took off till we touched down. As we were deplaning, they hugged, and we all went our separate ways. I rolled my eyes, a common occurrence during that time, as she shared with me facts about his life and military service as if she had known him for years.

"I'm looking for an opportunity in DC, Mike," I said on our call. I wish I could replay the rest of the conversation, seeing how important it was to the next decade of my life. But my memory is fuzzy. Often, we don't recognize a catalyst as it is happening. With distance comes understanding. Time removes the haze and makes it easy to see the chain of events that led you to where you are.

From that call, Mike made one introduction. That introduction led to a consulting gig, which became a full-time job. Upon submitting proof of that full-time job to the judge, he granted permission almost immediately for me and the coolest kid on the planet to move to Washington, DC. After two lawyers, three months in court, and an additional four months of commuting from MA to DC for the consulting gig, I was free to start over.

One introduction changed the trajectory of my life; it can for you too.

6

NETWORKING IS LIKE SEX

"Crazy-busy" is a great armor, it's a great way for numbing. What a lot of us do is that we stay so busy, and so out in front of our life, that the truth of how we're feeling and what we really need can't catch up with us.

—BRENÉ BROWN

Networking is like sex.

Everyone assumes everyone else knows how to do it. Some people are probably great at it. Others pretend they are. But we mainly do it wrong initially and only get good at it through self-understanding, communication, and practice.

No one ever teaches you how to network. We are all supposed to do it without guidance, support, or best practices. We are thrown into the professional world expected to make our way through a turbulent economy and a work world that looks different than it did for previous generations. Algorithms are sorting winning job applications based on keywords, and AI is writing more effective résumés and cover letters than we can. Employers are posting jobs that aren't even available and getting over eight hundred applications. Plus, most jobs exist in the hidden job market and aren't even advertised publicly. It's a jungle out there!

With all that, the one thing that has stayed the same is that networking is still queen. The statistic changes based on what report you read, but they state that roughly 70 to 85 percent of people secure their jobs through networking. Although some like to disagree about these data points, no one argues that a strong network exponentially improves your career growth opportunity and the chances of getting a job. It doesn't mean you can stop filling out applications and dump ChatGPT; it simply means that if you want to secure a new job, get promoted, start a business, or create a new work opportunity, you need strong, engaged, and supportive business relationships now.

* * *

We need people. Okay, that's a super obvious statement, and I am not a sociologist here, but we can all agree that other people have always been essential to our health, well-being, safety, and security.

6

The value of building solid relationships is a familiar concept to us, but the work of doing so gets lost in the maintenance of living. A consequence of our time-blocked, overworked, and busy-as-a-badge-of-honor lives is that we lose touch with the broad community of people that have mattered in our life, and we don't make the time to meet new people. This "lack of time" pushes us into a pattern of only engaging with the same couple of connections. Outsourcing our relationships to an algorithm, we allow social media to take over our friendships, choosing who we see when on our feed, believing that a DM, like, or comment is enough to indicate our care or interest.

Our lives are consumed with working; running a family; and ensuring kids are fed, bathed, and don't stick their finger in a socket. We try to make it to yoga but end up sitting in the parking lot at Starbucks instead, watching movie trailers on YouTube to decompress. With our labor spread so thin, how can we keep track of all our relationships? That's what Instagram is for, right?

Wrong!

Instagram is for practicing envy, feeding your FOMO, spending money on things you don't need, and stoking your anxiety. Instagram is not where you meaningfully catch up with past friends. You need to go old school and hop on a call or meet in person. The back-and-forth in the DMs is not a replacement for meaningful, one-on-one investment of your dedicated time and attention.

Here's what management expert Dr. Henry Mintzberg wrote in *Harvard Business Review*:

> Social media certainly connects us to whoever is on the other end of the line, and so extends our social networks in amazing ways. But this can come at the expense of deeper personal relationships. When it feels like we're up-to-date on our friends' lives through Facebook or Instagram, we may become less likely to call them, much less meet up. Networks connect; communities care.[10]

When social media takes over the management of our relationships, we are lulled into a false sense of belonging. We feel connected and disconnected simultaneously, which feeds our desire to stay on social media. It is a vicious cycle that keeps us from picking up the phone and hearing the other person's voice.

Yes, I said phone. You know, that thing Alexander Graham Bell invented back in the day that allows us to talk to people worldwide? Then Steve Jobs turned it into a computer that does super cool shit, the least important of which is allowing us to talk to people worldwide. We have outsourced our communication for efficiency and the promise of connection but feel more disconnected than ever. That would change if we just started picking up the phone and calling people.

---

10. Henry Mintzberg, "We Need Both Networks and Communities," *Harvard Business Review*, October 5, 2015, https://hbr.org/2015/10/we-need-both-networks-and-communities.

"Who has time for that?" you say.

You do! If you want to change your life, find new opportunities and build your dream work life. *You* have time for it.

You indicate your priorities by what you spend your time on and what you give your attention to. If you want to leave a toxic workplace, have more time for your family, and/or make more money, spending two and a half hours a day scrolling social media won't get it done. Your connections and conversations with the people in your life will. You get to choose which is more deserving of your time and attention.

As journalist and author Lois Wyse put it, "A good friend is a connection to life—a tie to the past, a road to the future, the key to sanity in a totally insane world."[11] Our relationships are the conduit to a whole and engaged life. What does that whole and engaged life look like to you? What does it feel like? Are you in it right now or dreaming about it? Or are you consumed by the insane world, hoping for a bit of sanity?

Let's be clear: your work serves the whole and engaged life you want, not vice versa. You are meant to work to *live*, not live to *work*, no matter what @lamborghinibro42 and @bossbabeperfectmomof12 tells you on Instagram (these are not real accounts, by the way). I know that is not the culture of

---

11. I couldn't find a solid source for this Lois Wyse quote, but here it is on Goodreads: https://www.goodreads.com/quotes/160017-a-good-friend-is-a-connection-to-life---a.

work we have been bred into in the United States. But it is the culture of work you can choose. So, what does working to live look like to you? What kind of life do you want? What world of work fits that life?

Maybe you want to spend more time with the people you love and need a more flexible work environment. Perhaps you dream of backpacking with your pug and living the self-employed, digital nomad lifestyle. You may want to make more money, be challenged, and have more responsibility in your company. Maybe you are tired of striving for a work culture that doesn't align with your values. You might be looking for a bicoastal lifestyle or the freedom to live abroad and need a job that supports that. Maybe you want to feel like you can breathe, leave your work at work at the end of the day, and have time for a couple of hobbies.

Amazingly, you can have any of those things or whatever you want. You just need to figure out wtf you want, share your hopes and dreams with your friends, family and connections, ask them for help when you need it, and go find or build the work adventure that supports that dream. It's not complicated. It can be difficult, but it isn't complex.

The equation looks like this:

WTF you want + share WTF you want = cool new opportunities that move you toward WTF you want

The same is true for the people who share their dreams with you. They figure out what they want, they share it with you, and you share ideas or opportunities to help them get there. It's a reciprocal process. We share our hopes, dreams, knowledge, insight, and opportunities, and we help each other.

But that's the hard part, isn't it—figuring out what you want. No matter what influencers or motivational gurus tell you, stopping long enough to identify what you want is complicated. More difficult still is disrupting your routine, your lifestyle, or the spoken or unspoken agreements you have with those around you in order to take the actions necessary to achieve what you want.

Our lives are full of patterns, people, circumstances, and expectations that organize and define our lives. Before we can stop and ask ourselves, "Hey, what do I want?" our life is overflowing with responsibilities and interpersonal dynamics. It doesn't mean we don't want some of these responsibilities. It does mean we don't often stop to ask ourselves whether we do or not—*partly* because we don't think we have the time and *mostly* because we don't want to know the answer. Because if we know the answer, we may have to do something about it.

* * *

Remember when your mom would ask, "If your best friend jumped off a building, would you do it too?" I always found it a ridiculous question. Of course I wouldn't jump off a building just because Erin (my childhood best friend) wanted to. I'd call Erin to see if she was okay or ask my mom if she had heard something terrible from Erin's dad. But after scrolling Instagram for twenty minutes, I think I need to change my whole business model based on what my feed tells me, or buy something because I'm spending too much time in leggings, whether I love leggings or not. #*stopthescroll*

We are naturally drawn to measuring ourselves based on what other people are doing and what other people will think. Our desire to fit in, belong, and be part of the crew is baked into our DNA. Back in the day, like way back in the day, we got eaten by bigger things than us if we didn't. Developing new relationships and asking for help is vulnerable, and if we can avoid it, we do. All of this bumps up against our desire to be comfortable and safe and avoid the four-hundred-pound feline licking its lips behind us.

What does all of this have to do with networking?

Everything.

"Networking" is just a word: the verb that puts the noun, your "network," into action. Okay, "networking" isn't officially a verb, but it should be. It adds intention and momentum to your network when it is essential to moving your career goals forward. It is a word that elicits complicated feelings and requires a set of actions that repels some and attracts others.

Some think it's a dirty word.

I'm a fan of dirty words. I enjoy dropping an F-bomb occasionally to help get my point across. And those who know me well know my humor can turn a little raunchy with the help (or excuse) of a couple of well-earned cocktails.

My mother tried her best to teach my brother and me appropriate language, but then Dad would come home and mention some asshole at work or the shitstorm that had come down. *She didn't scold* him, I thought, *so why should I avoid those words?* It made no sense to my developing brain. So, if you are offended by the occasional "inappropriate" language in this book, let me know, and I'll send you my dad's email. You can complain to him. He will probably respond to your email with a polite "Thank you for reading Maryann's book; I fucking love her."

Networking makes people feel a certain way, as if it requires you to be inauthentic or transactional. It can feel salesy, which comes with all this negative crap associated with it. In his bestselling book *To Sell Is Human*, author Daniel Pink conducted a survey where he asked people to state the first word that came to mind when they heard "sales" or "selling." Of the twenty-five most common words people thought of, 80 percent had negative connotations: words like pushy, difficult, yuck, sleazy, boring, manipulative, dishonest, and (my favorite) "ugh."

If networking feels salesy to you, of course you hate it! But networking isn't about selling; it's about sharing, communicating, and connecting. It is about building and nurturing relationships, prioritizing getting to know people, caring for them, and understanding what makes them tick and what they want for their future. Your network is simply a beautiful and remarkable collection of people from all corners of your life and experiences. It is a group of people interested in who you are and what you do.

You already know a ton of people. Some you may not want to see again. Like that guy who always stood too close to me in the office hallway, making awkward conversation. I'm okay not seeing him again. But there are a whole bunch of people you really enjoyed spending time with and aren't in touch with anymore for one reason or another. We lose sight of childhood friends, college friends, mom friends, book club pals, that person you met on the plane and connected with on LinkedIn, friendly ex-partners, family, past or current work colleagues. It is easy for those connections to fade away. But here is the exciting part: that one introduction that will change your life will come from someone you already know, not someone you just met.

With other people to support, advise, and help us, we grow and change. If we stay encased in our "crazy-busy" armor, as Brené Brown describes it, we keep ourselves from the belonging that one-on-one connection brings as well as from the wider world of opportunity.

7

RÉSUMÉS ARE A CRAPPY WAY OF MEASURING YOUR SKILLS

On average, employers look at résumés for six to seven seconds.

—INDEED

"But how will you make any money doing music and art?"

I was blessed with parents who never asked me this question, even though artistic endeavors consumed my first twenty-five years. Musical theater was my major as an undergrad at the University of Michigan, not because of Broadway ambitions but due to my love of singing and disinterest in studying opera.

My memories don't include dreams of a professional life as a performer, nor did my college studies venture into teaching how to do such a thing. Michigan taught me how to *do* the job of a performer but not necessarily how to *get* the job or any other job for that matter.

After graduation, I dutifully migrated to New York City like most of my friends. Open call after open call followed, and so did small showcases in the East Village before it became a trendy place to live, invites to agents, and my growing suspicion that this life didn't fit. I'd watch my friends, who all dreamed of being in front of the footlights, and wonder what was wrong with me. I continued to audition out of what felt like obligation, not desire. *That's what I'm supposed to do, right?* I thought.

Between auditions, I would put on musical cabarets or plays to provide myself and my friends with an opportunity to perform. Think Judy Garland and Mickey Rooney "let's put on a show" movies but set in New York City in the mid-1990s and early aughts in theaters across the street from peep shows and strip clubs.

I loved taking on the role of producer and director. It utilized my organizational, managerial, and creative skills, challenging me in a way that performing never did. It also helped that I was great at it. "It's just a side gig," I would tell myself, reminding me not to veer off course. Then, a surprising thing happened.

After a busy week of auditioning, I stepped in to sing for the casting director of the original production of *Beauty and the Beast* on Broadway. He nodded in recognition, and after my song, he said, "Hi, Maryann. I really love your voice, and you know I like you, but you are just too damn tall. I could never cast you as Belle." A little jarred in the moment, I smiled and said thank you and took my five-foot-nine frame out the door, down the elevator, and to the street. I waited to get upset or angry. Sad maybe? Some reaction that would reinforce the blow he had dealt. But nothing happened. All I felt was relief.

I had an epiphany that day. So many factors are out of my control as a performer, being at the whim of casting directors, producers, and directors who decide my professional fate. And in the end, it was possible none of it had anything to do with my talent or skill. I could be just "too damn tall." I asked myself, *Do I want a job dependent on something I have no control over? Do I want my career aspirations enmeshed with the interests and affinities of other people?* That audition, the casting director's kind honesty, my lack of ambition as a performer, and my growing interest in producing led me to change course.

From that day on, my full attention went into producing and directing. Singing became something to do in small clubs and lounges around the city for fun. My goals as an entrepreneur grew as my skills at raising money, creating and implementing a vision, managing teams of creatives, and marketing improved. Over the years, we grew to have two companies, one for-profit and one nonprofit, producing shows regionally and off Broadway. We helped to develop shows for regional theaters out of town by producing workshops for funders. We even had an internship program that brought students into town and provided them a place to stay in NYC while they worked for our start-up. It was an exciting roller-coaster ride I am grateful for.

After years of building and growing, and watching the changing economics of theater in NYC, my desire and excitement for the theater world waned. If I wanted to grow further, I could either bring in more investment and staff to scale my operations or shut down and work for one of the more extensive production companies. Neither felt like a good fit. I was four months pregnant and burned out from the grind, so after a decade in New York City, the companies were sundowned, and we left for a new adventure in western Massachusetts.

* * *

I have had a strange and circuitous career, drawing on a unique set of skills that take advantage of my ability to take action, find or make jobs for myself within companies, and build partnerships that help people improve their own opportunities. I'm an entrepreneur at heart, and after my producing career, I have spent over twenty years working for governments, institutions, and brands, bringing together billion-dollar partners and leveraging their resources to support thousands of people in getting jobs, accessing free therapy, and growing their businesses. I have enjoyed the grind, the challenge of aligning the right partners, getting to know the people at the helm of those complex organizations, and building the trust necessary to make a significant impact. It has kept my mind active, my curiosity fed, and my skills sharp.

Whether as a producer in New York City or in the positions I've held after, around the five-year mark, my career growth would stall and the frustration would settle in. Working harder and saying yes to more responsibility never solved that problem. I would gratefully take the promotions offered, but end up miserable and return to a familiar refrain, berating myself in the process.

What is your problem? Why can't you want what you have? I would scold myself. *The mayor just appointed you to a pretty cool gig that a lot of other people wanted; why don't you want it? Get on board and like it, dammit.* It was a reproduction of my interior monologue while auditioning in New York City.

I tried to like it, to want what other people wanted. *Isn't this what career growth looks like?* I'd ask myself. *Bigger jobs with better pay and higher status?* It is clear that for some, it is, and for others, it isn't—for me, it wasn't. It hadn't occurred to me then that career growth was personal, not universal. What felt like growth for me could be different than what growth was for someone else.

My satisfaction with work has rarely aligned with my promotions or the status of the positions I've held. It depends on whether the work is challenging, requires me to grow personally and professionally, whether I feel valued by those I work for, and the kind of impact I can have in the community I serve. My satisfaction and the quality of my work rely on the fit.

Back in 2021, fed up with the conversation about career advancement, journalist Bridget Thoreson went viral, tweeting, "I'm rejecting the career ladder metaphor in favor of the career river." She went on to offer multiple reasons why. "The ultimate goal of the career ladder is: reach the top," she tweeted. "The ultimate goal of the career river is: reach your ocean—a thriving, wide-open ecosystem fed by other rivers to explore."[12]

I could never have planned my career path ahead of time. But through the glaring beam of hindsight, it is clear how all the opportunities have fed each other into an ecosystem of relationships and opportunities that grew into a wicked, extraordinary career so far. Whether class III or class IV rapids, thankfully, all rivers have led me to the ocean I'm in now. It's pretty damn cool to sit on the other side of the previous twenty-plus years and think, *Yeah, that makes sense. I see how that happened, how you used that skill there, and leveraged that experience to find the next thing. What a ride!*

* * *

---

12. Bridget Thoreson (@BridgetThoreson), "I'm rejecting the career ladder metaphor in favor of the career river," Twitter, August 27, 2021, https://twitter.com/BridgetThoreson/status/1431286648495607808.

Résumés are an incomplete way of measuring our skills and value as potential employees. Yet they are the standard practice and too often serve as hiring managers' first impression. They are fed into an applicant tracking system (ATS), which weeds out unqualified applicants based on preprogrammed criteria and spits the *qualified* one to those with only six to seven seconds to spare.

For much of my career, my résumé was a patchwork of experience that didn't even make sense to me; how would it make sense to someone scanning it cold? It read like a Mad Libs story played between me and the Magic 8 Ball, with nouns, verbs, adjectives, and adverbs bouncing around each other, trying to find a place that makes sense. I had built my own companies, worked for universities, collaborated with cities, taught college, and even worked for a talent agent. My skills made me agile; my impact was clear, but none of it fit neatly into a specific job title. My confidence in my ability was high, but my Mad Libs résumé couldn't get me in front of the right people. What *could* were my relationships.

My experience is not unique. So many of us have eclectic work histories. We have switched careers, zigged instead of the expected zag, taken a career break to raise kids, followed a spouse overseas, or felt disillusioned with what we were doing and jumped into an entirely new thing. Trying to capture that river ride on one sheet of paper, add all the necessary keywords, and get through the ATS hoping to earn more than those six to seven seconds of attention feels impossible.

We certainly need to try. Résumés aren't going away anytime soon, but we can shift our priorities, and like that popular kid in school everyone always fawned over, we can stop giving it so much attention. The résumé is one of many ways to showcase your impact and experience but certainly not the best way. The solution is not to game the system with hours of rewrites and strategically placing the right words throughout; it is to demote the résumé from its role as the first impression. Those words on the page are one-dimensional and limited in their ability to tell the full story of who you are and the impact you deliver—so stop letting them try. That story requires a three-dimensional approach, which we will outline in the book's second half.

Until then, remember, you are more than what is on that piece of paper; your experience has value beyond your job titles. The keywords of others do not define the quality you bring to the opportunity, and you are so much more than only six to seven seconds can capture.

8

BLAME THE SYSTEM, NOT YOURSELF

Women have learned the language of men—have lived in the house of men—all their lives. We can speak it. You know when you learn a language, you learn French, you learn Spanish, it isn't your language until you dream in it, and the only way to dream in it is to speak it. And women speak men. But men don't speak women; they don't dream in it.

—MERYL STREEP

The first problem for all of us, men and women, is not to learn, but to unlearn.

—GLORIA STEINEM

Once, during a camping trip with my cousins out in Montana, I started wandering off, wasn't paying attention, and slid partially down a ravine. As my ten- or eleven-ish body landed on a lip of dirt and grass roughly twenty-five feet down, I remember thinking, *Well, shit. This isn't good.* I looked down, then up. Down looked like a poor option. Up seemed a better bet, including branches and earth that looked like they could hold my weight. I started climbing. No one was there to see me flop myself over the top a few minutes later, which was preferable because I wouldn't have wanted the fuss. I brushed myself off and started walking back toward camp. Throughout the sticky situation, I don't remember ever thinking, *I should call for help.*

* * *

"What are you going to do about it?" was a running theme in my childhood. If I was bored or didn't know what to do and asked my parents to point me toward something fun, I was told, "Boredom is a lack of imagination; go figure it out yourself." If I had a problem that needed a solution, they simply asked, "What are *you* going to do about it?" My parents didn't discourage asking for help, but they expected me to try to solve things myself before seeking the solution from them. Self-direction and autonomy were the priority. Sometimes, I just wanted someone to tell me what to do. But when I was told what to do, I rebelled. You can imagine the conflict. Damn, people are complicated, aren't they?

8

Asking for help is daunting, especially in a culture that prizes self-reliance. And if you are a recovering control freak like me, asking for help makes your skin itch. When asked why asking for help is so hard, Stanford social psychologist Xuan Zhao said, "Some people may fear that asking for help would make them appear incompetent, weak, or inferior." She added that some people are "concerned about being rejected, which can be embarrassing and painful," and that "others may be concerned about burdening and inconveniencing others."[13]

How many of those items above reflect how you feel? Do you feel weak asking for help? Or worry about bothering people? Are you afraid the people you ask will say no? Our desire to avoid the discomfort of those feelings keeps us isolated, stuck, or championing the incorrect belief that going it alone makes us stronger. Vulnerability is a bitch, but it is also the gateway to deeper relationships, better opportunities, and a richer life.

Our beliefs and attitudes about asking for help or advocating for ourselves develop from our family, social conditioning, and personal experiences. These beliefs impact the way we think, and the way we think determines what we do.

What is your family story? Did your parents have strong feelings one way or another about people who needed help? Did they consider people lazy for not helping themselves, or worthy of

---

13. Melissa De Witte, "Asking for help is hard, but people want to help more than we realize, Stanford scholar says," *Stanford News*, September 8, 2022, https://news.stanford.edu/2022/09/08/asking-help-hard-people-want-help-realize/.

support because everyone needs help now and then? Were you encouraged to talk about yourself or your accomplishments? Were your opinions sought after, or did they create tension in the house. Were you empowered to speak up, or told to be seen and not heard?

Layered on top of our family and personal experience is a smack-ton of social conditioning. In their book *Women Don't Ask*, authors Linda Babcock and Sara Laschever wrote:

> Women are less likely than men to negotiate for themselves for several reasons. First, they often are socialized from an early age not to promote their own interests and to focus instead on the needs of others... Women tend to assume that they will be recognized and rewarded for working hard and doing a good job. Unlike men, they [women] haven't been taught that they can ask for more.[14]

Asking for what you want and asking for more, especially if it falls outside traditional gendered expectations, is discombobulating. As women ask for more, own their career advancement, and opt out of or redesign conventional gender expectations, they are fighting through generations of social conditioning. This history of gendered raising—the subtle and not-so-subtle prescribing of what is appropriate for women to do or not do, to say, sound like, look like, be like, or identify as—

---

14. Linda Babcock and Sara Laschever, *Women Don't Ask: The High Cost of Avoiding Negotiation—and Positive Strategies for Change* (New York: Bantam, 2007).

has an impact on how we feel about ourselves and how others treat us in return. It shapes what we feel we can and cannot have, and what we want or will accomplish.

Babcock and Laschever also stated, "Even when women can imagine changes that might increase their productivity at work, their happiness at home, or their overall contentment with their lives, their suppressed sense of entitlement creates real barriers to their asking."[15]

Our discomfort with asking for help is normal. So are doubt and insecurity. Shit, I feel doubt and discomfort all the time. About whether I am doing the right thing, how much money I'm making, and whether I will ever find a kind, funny, curious, emotionally available dude my age. No matter how normal the discomfort is, it still sucks.

This internal and external pressure to be confident, believe in yourself, have it all under control, fight for women's rights and animal rights, and save the planet while also taking it upon yourself to get the card signed by everyone at the office before Frank's retirement cake arrives is intense. We feel the need to be everything to everybody, to take on their emotional labor while suppressing our own. We get mad at ourselves for struggling with self-doubt and insecurity. *If I just believed in myself*, we think, *if I just went for it, or if I knew my worth—if I could just fix myself—I'd be better.*

---

15. Babcock and Laschever, *Women Don't Ask*.

The truth is you are not the problem; the problem is the system we developed within. You don't need to be better or different. It's time to stop blaming yourself, and blame the system instead.

Our confidence is not delivered through our DNA. It is not something that the lucky few inherit through their genes, and the rest of us are shit out of luck, struggling to make up for what was missing in our genetic code. Yes, some people may struggle less with insecurity or doubt, or be more naturally inclined toward confidence; it may come easier for them. But that doesn't mean you can't learn it, and it doesn't mean that those who seem confident don't suffer from self-doubt as well.

Here are a few things to keep in mind about confidence:

Confidence is a skill, not a trait.
Like any skill, we can develop it, practice it, and deploy it when and where we need it. We can build it. Confidence gets better through practice and performance, through trial and error. Like all other skills, the more we commit to that practice and performance, the more we can master them.

Confidence is not contingent on your belief in yourself.
Confidence comes from the Latin word *fidere*, which means "to trust." At its core, confidence is the state of feeling certain about something—trusting *something*. The key is defining what that *something* is.

We put enormous pressure on ourselves to be the container of that something, believing we are what we need to trust. We think we hold all the power, that if we just trust and believe in ourselves, anything is possible. This is a lot of pressure! It makes our confidence reliant on a cocktail of high self-esteem, positive self-talk, and killer self-promotion.

Improving our self-esteem, limiting negative self-talk, and increasing our ability to promote ourselves are vital skills to work on. They are crucial to improving our professional and personal lives. But requiring them to fuel our confidence puts an unnecessary burden on us all. It adds a barrier of entry to progress, and it can stop us in our tracks.

Sometimes our self-esteem is flying high; sometimes our doubt gets the best of us. Sometimes we can ask for what we need and promote our accomplishments, and other times, we kick ourselves for failing miserably to do all of that. Our experiences of self-esteem, self-doubt, self-talk, and self-promotion are emotional, and they ebb and flow. When we put our confidence in the hands of that emotional roller coaster, we set ourselves up for a ride that doesn't provide the stability we need to reach our goals.

There are historical, cultural, and social systems at play.

There are historical, cultural, and social systems at play that have kept women from having access to opportunity. Our self-worth largely develops due to the value placed on our presence in society and the roles we are expected to play.

Our actions and choices have been historically confined, structured, and limited. Although we have made progress, here are some sobering reminders:

- Laws that kept married women from employment were still in effect in the 1940s.
- The Equal Credit Opportunity Act wasn't passed until 1974, which means women couldn't access a business loan without the cosign of a man before that time.
- The racial wealth gap for women is dismal. According to an article in the American Bar Association's *Human Rights* magazine, "For every dollar of wealth owned by a single white man, single Black women and single Latinas own nine cents."[16]
- As CNN reported in early 2024: "At least 510 anti-LGBTQ bills were introduced in state legislatures across the United States last year—a new record, according to American Civil Liberties Union data. That's nearly three-times the number of such bills introduced in 2022."[17]

So, when navigating our confidence, our ability to self-promote, and our aversion to asking for help, it is essential to recognize that context matters.

---

16. Amy Royce and Amy Matsui, "Unsupported: Underinvestment in the Care Economy Drives Gender and Racial Wealth Gaps," *Human Rights*, vol. 48, no. 2 (2023), https://www.americanbar.org/groups/crsj/publications/human_rights_magazine_home/wealth-disparities-in-civil-rights/unsupported/.

17. Annette Choi, "Record Number of Anti-LGBTQ Bills Were Introduced in 2023," CNN Politics online, updated January 22, 2024, https://www.cnn.com/politics/anti-lgbtq-plus-state-bill-rights-dg/index.html.

8

As Newton explained, objects in motion tend to stay in motion, and objects at rest stay put in that resting state. Women, or anyone who didn't fit the white-male model, were meant to remain at rest—were meant to stay in their place.

This history, this oppression, has had a generational impact on how we feel about ourselves and how others treat us in return. Placing our confidence in our belief in ourselves makes us think we're to blame when that belief wavers. We think our lack of confidence is our fault when it is certainly not.

When you spend your day in an environment where people overtly or inadvertently, consciously or subconsciously, push back against your dreams, goals, even your presence or how you identify, it deeply impacts what you think is possible. This isn't an excuse; it is a reality.

It is not your fault if you have a terrible week full of negative self-talk. It is not your fault if you struggle with self-limiting beliefs; it is perfectly understandable. Those feelings and beliefs will ebb and flow as you work to understand them and work through them—and as we change the systems perpetuating them. Our self-doubt has been nurtured. We have been surrounded by doubt every time we've stepped out of other people's expectations. So don't get mad at yourself when you feel self-doubt; get mad at all that systemic shit, and take action to build the life you want anyway.

Confidence comes from doing, not believing.

The standard approach to building confidence suggests that we must believe in ourselves to have confidence. Then, we can use that confidence to take action; those actions will then lead us to achieve our goals. This approach is backward.

Confidence follows action, not the other way around. When we take action toward our goals, depending on the results of those actions, we adjust and act again. As those actions lead to results, we develop confidence and trust that our actions will lead to success.

Remember that Latin word *fidere*: to trust. At its core, confidence is the state of trusting something. That something is action—we trust that action will lead to results. As we become more confident, we grow to believe that taking the right action achieves a positive outcome. This builds strength and confidence.

The more you take action *despite* your doubt and discomfort, the more confident you will become. Action leads to results, and results lead to more action, which leads to more confidence. Doubt and discomfort will still be there, but the action will start to inoculate you from its power. All of this is to remind you that you are not the problem. Give yourself a little breathing room, skip the judgment, and just take action.

9

FIFTEEN THOUSAND FEET TO FREEDOM

You wanna fly, you got to give up the shit that weighs you down.

—TONI MORRISON

Thanks to the introduction from Mike, I secured a part-time consulting gig at the George Washington University, assessing the operations, staff, and programming of their performance venue and then creating a redevelopment plan. I ended up managing the staff as well. We redesigned the programming, budgeting, technology, marketing, and internal venue operational systems during my tenure. We hired staff, increased production, generated partnerships, and hosted the filming of nationally aired programming. My child, who was nine at the time, also helped at the box office now and then when the boss wasn't watching.

My boss was a prickly guy; there was something warm about him on the inside, which unfortunately wasn't very accessible on the outside. Every so often, I'd want to (gently) knock him on the head to crack the shell and see if that warmer center would come out to play. Demanding, and impertinent at times, he had a clear idea of how he wanted things done, and I didn't always do what he wanted. "Maryann," he said to me, irritated, "you go 200 percent when you buy into what we are doing, but when you don't, you only move 50 percent." I took the feedback as a compliment, which he didn't intend it to be. His point was for me to get off my ass and do what I was told, whether I believed in it or not.

I've been around many different leaders and leadership styles in my lifetime, whether working for, collaborating with, or being raised by them. Some engendered exceptional work from their team but at the expense of caring about the toll their demands took. Others cared too much about the personal lives of those who worked for them, which undercut the leaders' ability to challenge workers to do their best work. A couple have been so focused on their own visibility and ego that they've alienated the many people who made their success possible.

Some leaders are exceptional at conveying vision, while others find it less important or lack the communication skills to motivate, inspire, or even articulate that vision. I find it difficult to do my best work when the mission, whether developed by me or others, is unclear. It's hard to know what to *do* when you don't know *the why*. It's hard to know *the why* if you don't define it or no one ever communicates it to you.

I am not unique in my desire for purpose. Research from McKinsey & Company indicated that 70 percent of employees surveyed said that "their personal sense of purpose is defined by their work."[18] And *Harvard Business Review* published a study saying that nine out of ten workers are "willing to earn less money" to do more meaningful work.[19] For better or worse, our work is a part of our identity. And if we spend ninety thousand hours at work during our lifetime, as is commonly stated, it should mean something.

As my consulting term was coming to an end, the university floated the full-time job I had been advocating for and had written into the redevelopment plan. They held a ghost application process, as they were required to do, and they interviewed other candidates for the job I was promised/not promised. I had done this dance before and would do it again.

---

18. Naina Dhingra et al., "Help Your Employees Find Purpose—or Watch Them Leave," McKinsey & Company, April 5, 2021, https://www.mckinsey.com/capabilities/people-and-organizational-performance/our-insights/help-your-employees-find-purpose-or-watch-them-leave.

19. Shawn Achor et al., "9 Out of 10 People Are Willing to Earn Less Money to Do More-Meaningful Work," *Harvard Business Review*, November 06, 2018, https://hbr.org/2018/11/9-out-of-10-people-are-willing-to-earn-less-money-to-do-more-meaningful-work?registration=success.

Here's how it tends to go:

- Employers create a job for me, for which I write the job description.
- They make it clear they are legally required to do a search, but they install me in the position with all rights and responsibilities as the search commences.
- I send in a résumé and cover letter for the job, and I interview with the other candidates.
- At the end of the search process, they provide an offer for the job I've already been doing for a couple of months, and they onboard me into the position I already hold.

When my boss finally gave me the offer letter that confirmed my full-time job, he looked at me, confused by my lack of excitement. I was strung so tight, on the verge of biting someone's head off or crying most of the time, and exhausted from my schedule, commuting back and forth from MA to DC. I thanked him, left his office, and immediately called my lawyer, shaking.

From July, when I started the consulting gig, until December, when we moved to DC for good, my routine included a weekly four-hundred-mile commute from MA to DC and twelve-hour workdays while on site. Since my ex-husband and I split time equally, while my child was with their dad, I was in DC, and when they were with me, I was in MA. I would get up at 3:00 in the morning each week to shower and pack my child's lunch. Sue Ellen, a dear friend, would arrive at 4:00 a.m. to ensure the little lovebug got up, ate breakfast, and made it to school on time. I'd drive an hour to Hartford, catch the 6:00 a.m. flight to Baltimore, grab the train to DC, and go straight to my job. After half the week in DC, I would take the train back to Baltimore, fly back to Hartford, drive to MA, and pick up my child. A couple of days later, the cycle would repeat all over again, for the entire five and a half months.

Along with the stress of a custody case, the demands of my consulting gig, and adjusting to a new parenting schedule, I was a jumble of raw thoughts and feelings, trying to take action while struggling to find balance on the wobble board that was my life. And to top it off, I had to fucking get on a plane twice a week to keep my consulting gig.

I hate to fly. I believe with every fiber of my being that I am not meant to be in the air. I do it because my desire for experiences near and far is stronger than my fear of flying. The airplane is a necessary evil that gets me where I want to go, no matter how awful it feels.

Once, while I was commuting, as the TSA agent checked my ID and boarding pass, he said, "Sweetie, this ticket is for BWI."

"Yep, I know," I said. "I'm heading to BWI."

"No, dear," he replied, "this is a ticket from BWI to Hartford for this morning." I didn't quite understand what he was saying.

I looked at the ticket, confused. "You will need to talk to the ticketing agent," he continued.

I stepped out of the line, handed my boarding pass to the agent, and explained that I needed to get on the 6:00 a.m. flight to BWI, which was what I had done every week. She could tell I wasn't at my best, and thankfully decided to take pity on me. I like to believe she saw something familiar—that overwhelm we feel as we watch the balls drop around us as we fail to do everything right, *I suck at this* streaming like ticker tape across our forehead. She typed a bit, I mumbled a few answers to her questions, and then she calmly explained that I had booked a month of travel backward. Instead of flying from Hartford to Baltimore and back to Hartford every week, I had booked my flights from Baltimore to Hartford and back to Baltimore every week.

What transpired next was underscored by one of those intense, calm cries: no heaving or wailing, just tears streaming down my face while trying to absorb what the ticket agent was telling me. I stared at her, not wholly understanding what she had said. "I did what?" I asked. "I'm supposed to fly to Baltimore this morning."

"Yes," she responded. "We can fix this."

"What?" I said, stunned.

"We can fix this," she replied calmly. And she did. This angel in light blue with her neck scarf tied neatly in a double-wrap

9

French knot rebooked all my flights and got me on a flight half an hour later. I thanked her, composed myself, and headed back to security.

Even though airplanes are a tool of the devil, I grew to love the airport. As exhausting as the pace of my schedule was, between the moment I stepped inside Bradley International Airport in Hartford until I arrived at Union Station in DC, I was in an alternate world. Unreachable and protected. There was nothing to do and no one to respond to. I wasn't required to explain myself, solve other people's problems, or pretend to be okay. I could sit in limbo—in between where I was and where I wanted to be—pop a lorazepam as needed, and escape. Time stopped for those moments, giving me space to breathe and relax, during which I read every Vince Flynn novel I could find.

I still feel calm when I step into an airport. No matter the chaos, I have no control or responsibility once inside. All that is required is to make it to my gate, get on the plane, and deplane upon landing. If the plane is delayed, screening is backed up, or the Starbucks on Concourse B doesn't have mobile-ordering capability and the line is too long, it's okay. I accept it as is. The things that might stress me out in the real world just don't have the same power in the airport.

Back in DC, when my boss handed me the offer letter, I didn't know how to respond. I had been walking the line between following up and pestering about it for months. Every day without an offer, I was terrified to get a call from my lawyer saying the judge had ruled unequivocally that I could never leave the state and would be entombed in some patriarchal dungeon for women who dared to dream big. So when it was safely in my hands, I called my lawyer. She screamed in excitement for me, sent it to the court, and the judge ruled we could leave the state immediately.

I was free.

* * *

Certain experiences require you to rewrite your beliefs about yourself. We can get so attached to the stories we tell ourselves that we forget to check in to see if they are true. We can think we aren't capable, strong, or brave, but as Brené Brown says, "Sometimes the bravest and most important thing you can do is just show up."[20] Show up at the airport and get on the plane. Show up for yourself and leave a relationship that is hurting you. Show up for your desire to be fulfilled, and seek a work opportunity that values and challenges you. Show up and ask someone else for help.

And maybe hurtling through the sky at five-hundred miles per hour and fifteen thousand feet, in what amounts to a double-decker bus weighing nine hundred thousand pounds, is what carries you to freedom.

---

20. Brené Brown, *Daring Greatly: How the Courage to Be Vulnerable Transforms the Way We Live, Love, Parent, and Lead* (New York: Avery, 2015).

9

The pathway of your life can be traced through the people who weave in and out of it, those who participate, whether close up or from a distance, and the ones who offer their support. Those who help may not be the people you expect. They may be difficult and complicated or dealing with their own shit. It could be a demanding boss, a kind ticketing agent, or a family friend with the right connections. The key is to be open to whomever they are and be grateful for their support however it shows up.

10

I CAN SEE THE TOP OF THE WASHINGTON MONUMENT FROM MY CLASSROOM

A year from now, you will wish you had started today.

—KAREN LAMB

The move to DC happened quickly. It helped that I already had a house to move into, thanks to my impulsivity. Our understated brick row house with a stoop was settled on a tree-lined street within walking distance of the local elementary school. The emptiness of the interior was broken up by a couch, one mattress upstairs, and a fresh coat of paint. Where our previous living arrangement was cavernous, our new home was cozy.

My routine in DC while commuting was simple. After work, I returned to the house, taped another room to prepare for painting, walked over to the closest restaurant, grabbed a glass of wine and something to eat, and walked back to my empty house to paint. This ritual of taping and painting gave me something uncomplicated to count on and control—something simple to fix and improve. The work to heal myself would take much longer, but painting those walls was a great start.

As anthropology professor and author Dimitris Xygalatas wrote in his book *Ritual*, because of their "highly structured and reliably predictable nature," rituals "serve as an anchor in the storm that is our world." He went on to say that by "providing a sense of order and control over the frequently disorderly and uncontrollable situations we face in our daily lives, they help us cope with anxiety."[21] To paint, I had to secure the tape, lay the drop cloth, pour the paint, affix the roller, dip the roller into the paint, and roll up and down the wall. Then repeat and repeat, until the new color took over. I'd stand back and look at the beautiful thing I had created. Clean, crisp, and free from bumps or bruises. There were no scars from furniture being moved or life being lived, just a blank wall with a satin finish. This new, pristine canvas was full of possibilities.

The offer letter came in November, and my child was in school in DC by January. The day we left MA, I took a picture of us standing behind our car. Our bikes, safely secured behind us,

---

21. Dimitris Xygalatas, *Ritual: How Seemingly Senseless Acts Make Life Worth Living* (New York: Little, Brown Spark, 2022).

framed our tired smiles. That picture sat in a small frame in the corner of the kitchen for ten years—a reminder of the beginning of our new adventure, of what is possible when I dream.

The difficulty wasn't over; it rarely is. I was thrilled to be moving. It was the reward for all my distress and determination. Where I was overjoyed, my child was not. They had navigated so much change in the preceding four years from our separation and divorce, losing their dog, and then moving to DC. They were leaving everything they knew, their dad and their friends.

"I hate DC. I don't know why we had to move here." This was a common refrain for the first couple of months. "Why do we have to walk everywhere? I don't like walking!" and "I don't know anyone. What am I supposed to do? You're making me have to make a whole new group of friends. I already have friends." And, of course, "I don't like this school. School sucks."

Or simply silence, which was the worst. To say they were pissed is an understatement.

* * *

One of the first things I had done upon moving into my parents' home was get a dog. When I was there alone, the silence was deafening. Without the day-to-day sounds of childhood adventures or a city soundtrack, I felt uneasy. The low hum of city sounds, of neighbors chatting, kids playing, or cars driving by is comforting to me. The sounds of nature? Not quite as much.

Health journalist Kirsten Nunez explains that nature is full of pink noise. "Pink noise consists of all frequencies we can hear, but the energy isn't equally distributed across them. It's more intense at lower frequencies, which creates a deep sound."[22] City noise felt like home to me. The pink noise drove me crazy. I would walk outside, and everything was weirdly quiet and loud at the same time. Crickets chirped, birds whistled, and there was rustling and scurrying—with deer, wild turkeys, and the occasional moose staring me down as if to ask, "WTF are you doing here? You don't belong." No shit. I was the outsider in that situation.

Our dog, Boo, was my lifeline. My buddy, someone to take care of me in simple ways. He broke up the quiet with the click-clacking of his nails on the hardwood floor and entertained me with his obsession for disemboweling any stuffed thing in sight—and as I cried, he lay his head on my lap. He needed me in uncomplicated ways I could manage, and I needed him desperately. My child and I loved him dearly.

Our social connections and enduring relationships are crucial to our well-being. And research shows that we form similar social bonds with our pets, especially dogs, as with our partners,

---

22. Kirsten Nunez, "What Is Pink Noise and How Does It Compare with Other Sonic Hues?", *Healthline*, updated March 10, 2023, https://www.healthline.com/health/pink-noise-sleep.

10

family, and friends. "Pet care and self-care are linked," explains academic and psychologist Dr. June McNicholas. "When you take a dog out for a walk, people talk to you and that may be the only social contact an isolated person has the whole day," she says. "When pet owners leave the house to buy pet food," she continues, "they're more likely to buy food for themselves and when they feed their pet, they'll sit down to eat too."[23]

As my commuting schedule continued, it was impossible to care for Boo without leaving him with house sitters half of the time. He was stressed, and I was overwhelmed; the best solution was for him to stay with my parents, who were living in Louisiana at the time, while I got my job shit figured out. Thankfully, my animal-loving mom and my "not-a-dog-person" dad agreed to take him. In reality they didn't have a choice; I told them they needed to take the dog, and they accepted the responsibility.

The day Boo was picked up for transport down south, my child sat on the front steps and wailed. They have always been full of big emotions, but I had yet to hear that sound come out of their compact little body. With snot flying and through sobs, they impaled me with words about how terrible, horrible, no good I was as a mother for sending their dog away. I sat there and let them stab away because they were right. I felt like an awful parent, a dreadful person, a failure. I wasn't just sending

---

23. Ann Robinson, "'Dogs Have a Magic Effect': How Pets Can Improve Our Mental Health," *Guardian*, March 17, 2020, https://www.theguardian.com/society/2020/mar/17/dogs-have-a-magic-effect-the-power-of-pets-on-our-mental-health.

their dog away; I was sending away my friend and constant companion, the one individual who provided me the consistent unconditional love I so desperately needed.

Thankfully, I sliced my palm open on an exposed iron sliver on the porch while trying to comfort my inconsolable child. The blood dripping down my arm interrupted the wail and created a reason to go inside and clean ourselves up.

As parents, we hold a contradiction in our hearts and our bodies. We must navigate the decisions, actions, and feelings of the day while also holding our hopes and desires for the future. Those two things can be in competition with each other. When our decisions for the future create pain in our children in the present, no matter how vital those choices are, it fucking sucks. We have to sit in the immediate impact of our decision while waiting for the long-term benefit. We think we "know what is best," but in truth we are only guessing.

Even when you believe the steps you are taking are right, you rarely get instant gratification that says, "Yep! Nicely done. Win one for the mom team!" We don't have a crystal ball that tells us if we do A, B, and C, that will produce exactly X, Y, and Z. The payoff and the outcome take time to develop. You have to wait, hoping that the future you are working toward will be better and less debilitating than the past. You have to have faith that you will get where you want to go. You hold that dream in your hand and take small actions daily to lead you there. Then one day, you look around and think, *Shit, look at where we are. Look at what I did. Look at what is possible.* But you rarely get there without moments on the front porch with your child screaming at you as you send the dog away.

Most change requires faith. We jump into the river and trust that our effort and the flow of the current will take us where we need to go. Whether you are building a new life after divorce or changing careers to support that new life, it is hard to know how it will go. Some of it you can control, be proactive, and invest your time and attention into—but the rest requires faith. Faith that you are doing the right thing.

*　　*　　*

About five or six months in, we were walking back from school, and my kid said, "Guess what."

"What?" I returned.

"I can see the top of the Washington Monument from my classroom."

"Really?"

"Yep," and after a pause, "that's kinda cool."

Fuck yeah, it's cool, I screamed in my head. But what came out of my mouth instead was, "That's great, baby."

It took them a while to warm up to DC, but once they did, they were off to the races: hanging out with new friends, pushing me to let them walk the neighborhood by themselves, discovering the freedom of the metro, and having their own adventures. They adapted and thrived.

Years later when we were driving to a college visit, they said, "I love DC."

"Me too," I said.

"I'm not sure I'd be the person I am today if we didn't move here," they continued.

"Me either," I responded.

11

MOM, YOU'RE KINDA LOW-KEY THRIVING

If we had no winter, the spring would not be so pleasant; if we did not sometimes taste of adversity, prosperity would not be so welcome.

—ANNE BRADSTREET

My child and I were quite the team for the next ten years. What I had imagined was wonderful, but what I hadn't imagined was better. If we stick to the plan, we only experience what we thought was possible at the moment the plan was created. But if we stay open and agile, our experiences and the people we meet along the way will expand our plan into a world we never could have pictured.

We built new routines and rituals, grew with a new community of friends, and found family. We traveled the world together. I faced the ups and downs of single-parenting with an unexpected ease. Not that it was easy, but it was what I wanted and had fought so hard for, so I was grateful for all that came with it. What seemed impossible before had become manageable. What seemed challenging became less of a burden and more of an adventure. It felt good to be in my skin, to see my life as a series of choices and opportunities, to realize that I could do hard things and it would be okay. That it would be more than okay, and that the other side of the hardship would be something beautiful.

Author and researcher Beronda L. Montgomery mentions in her book *Lessons From Plants* that the knowledge of plants shows us "you thrive or languish based on your ability to know who you are, where you are, and what you are supposed to be doing."[24] You don't need to know everything, but you do need to know something. Omniscience is not the goal; awareness and curiosity are.

Our lives cycle through seasons. There are moments of shedding, hibernation, birth, and regrowth. Without our fall or winter, we wouldn't have the possibilities that bloom and flourish in spring and summer. This cycle happens multiple times throughout our life, necessarily so, and it fuels our personal and professional growth. Our self-awareness and willingness to listen

---

24. Beronda L. Montgomery, *Lessons from Plants* (Cambridge, MA: Harvard University Press, 2021).

11

to what that self is telling us shepherd us through the cycle. Without it, we can get stuck in one season and never make it through.

Each season on its own, without the others, has its drawbacks. It's hard to imagine birth and regrowth being a bad thing, but left unchecked, the overgrowth leads to smothering everything around it. If we shed and get lost in hibernation, we might never come back to life.

* * *

Over time my work with the university grew stale. The challenge was gone. My leaders wanted me to maintain operations instead of growing the organization in ways that would excite me or take advantage of my unique skills. All of which led me to start looking elsewhere.

Fit comes and goes. It's weird for it not to. It is not a failure to outgrow something or to discover that your desires and needs have changed. The university gig was the perfect fit for the moment it represented. It provided the anchor necessary to start my postdivorce life. It offered a challenge I could sink my teeth into and a platform through which I could learn about my new home in DC.

My career has been built upon my strength in bringing people together and playing a matchmaker of sorts, filling in the gaps between where the organization I represent is and where they want to be, by building the partnerships and programs necessary to bridge that gap.

Through my work at the George Washington University, I met someone who worked for the Government of the District of Columbia. That conversation unlocked new interest and curiosity, as I discovered the challenges the city was facing in supporting their creative and entrepreneurial community. I began developing new relationships with government officials, providing advice and support from my previous years of creative-economy work. Those conversations and that support turned into a consulting gig and then a full-time post within the Government of the District of Columbia, and a further mayoral appointment to launch a new office for the District.

* * *

As they do, my kid grew up.

When you are at the beginning, with a child spitting up peas down the front of your shirt, eighteen years into the future seems hard to imagine. In hindsight though, those years pass in a heartbeat. I was staring down an empty nest, a strong desire to quit my government job for more freedom and independence, and a fiftieth birthday.

Everyone was aging. My kid, me, my parents, even Boo the dog. Boo stayed with my parents and followed them back to Massachusetts when they retired. He showered them with the love and affection he had shown us, became their constant companion and protector, and even took on a bear who wandered onto the front patio looking for birdseed one afternoon, receiving a claw-shaped swipe to his belly as a memento. When it was time to say goodbye to Boo, I sat petting his head and thanked him for the gift he had given to our entire family. The loss of Boo, another marker of time passing and the seasons changing.

I moved the picture that anchored the corner of the kitchen, the one of us the day we left MA for DC. I didn't need it as an empowering reminder anymore. It could take its place with the hundreds of other fun, beautiful, and meaningful memories captured, printed, and tacked to the wall in the upstairs hallway. I was staring at a new canvas, an emptying house, a bare corner of the counter, and endless opportunity.

As the frustration and burnout settled in with my work for the local government, and after I was scolded for missing a call from my boss because I was in the bathroom, I set the date to quit, gave notice a month or so later, and left.

I was starting over again.

* * *

There is an energy burst I feel in reinventing myself. I take comfort in the action it requires, but it gets a bit harder each time. The community you have surrounding you changes and adapts as you shed and prepare for that regrowth.

After leaving my government job, I spent a glorious amount of time with myself and my kiddo. After holding such a public position, it was a relief to sink back into a quieter space. The introvert in me took a year and a half to stretch her legs, breathe, and enjoy the silence. Over time, I started to feel the pull to get back to work, to build my business, to engage with the world again and reengage with my relationships. And I got another dog.

* * *

During an unusually quiet ride back home from college for the holiday break, I heard, "Mom?"

"Yes, baby." I said.

"You seem like you are low-key thriving right now."

I took a pause and said, "How do you feel about that, baby?"

"It's okay," they returned, unable to hide their mix of happy-for-me and pissed-I-wasn't-crumbling-without-them. I wasn't expecting to be doing as well as I was, but they were right, I was "low-key thriving."

I missed them terribly. From our yearly international adventures to game night at home, our conversations about life, the mundane day-to-day routine of sharing a home together, or just reading side by side. So much of my fun and adventure had included them. But I hadn't anticipated the emotional labor of day-to-day parenting that I would release in their absence. I had time and space to dream in new ways, to imagine how I might want to live this next stage of my life, and to breathe more deeply. I had been striving without a break for almost twenty years; it was time to think about what came next.

This new journey is a completely new landscape for my life, work, and hopefully love. No matter how well networked I am, starting over brings with it a whole new set of challenges and opportunities and people to connect with. But first, I had to ask myself, *What do I want (and what don't I want) this next ten years to look like?* The vision I had for the last ten years didn't apply anymore. My environment, responsibilities, lifestyle, relationships, child's needs, my needs, were all different.

I'm still working on what it all looks like, but here are a few things I already know:

I want to live a hustle-free life. Hard work doesn't bother me, but I am unwilling to burn myself out in the ways I have previously. I see "hustle" as a mindset as well as a set of behaviors that I don't want to participate in because it negatively impacts my health and well-being. As I figure out my limits in this new workflow, it might (or might not) take me longer to reach my goals, but I don't give a shit. My health must take precedence.

I want to prioritize my relationships. My parents are still around, are wicked cool, and I want to spend time with them while I have them. I have friends around the country I want to see more, and I want to build new personal and business relationships. I would also love to meet a fun, adventurous, emotionally available man my own age, which seems harder than it should be. Someone to complement my life, not complete it.

I want hobbies. I want to spend guilt-free time reading, creating, traveling, actually fixing shit in my house, doing fun stuff, learning new things, etc. I want to fill my nonwork time with nonwork things.

I want a thriving business that is lean and agile, that can adapt with me as I change and grow, and also as the needs of my community grow.

I want to build new wealth in terms of revenue, income, and assets that allow me to live well and to support my child—and whatever their family becomes—to live well in the future.

* * *

For my birthday recently, my child came to town and took me to see the band Sammy Rae & The Friends at the 9:30 Club here in DC. It was probably the best birthday present I can remember receiving. We had so much fun!

This empty-nesting thing is a crazy new world that feels equally thrilling and damn difficult. Spending that time with them reminded me that nothing feels quite as right, clear, and perfect as having an adventure with them. It showed me that what I am doing now is harder than I acknowledge. It's been twenty years since I've been this alone with my thoughts, wants, and needs—with the freedom to choose almost anything I might want to pursue.

Choice is a paradox. Liberating and confining at the same time. Too much choice makes it hard to make a decision. Too little choice makes us feel like we have no control over our lives. I am trying to be patient, knowing that it takes time to get comfortable with a new identity—this new life structure without them. Patience doesn't come naturally to me. But like confidence, it can be learned.

All of this to say that life shit is hard. There are brilliant days and bad days and everything in between. And that's okay.

*   *   *

I imagine you picked up this book because you are in the middle of, or seeking, a change. The process outlined in the next section of the book is the same process I have used to find or create my own career adventures, connect billion-dollar partners, and help hundreds of people find their own next right-fit opportunities. It is also the process I am going through right now.

This isn't something I am just teaching; it is something I am experiencing again, with you. Every time I reinvent myself, I return to this process. Every time, it leads me exactly where I am meant to be. This process can do the same for you, and I hope my journey can be a small reminder that those dreams you are sitting on, that feeling you have of wanting more—that desire to challenge yourself to live the life you want—is possible and nearer than you may imagine.

In the next section of the book, we are going to get tactical, break down this process into steps that you can put into action right now. Are you ready?

Let's get into Part 2!

Part Two

Part Two Introduction

I want you to leave Part 2 of this book with practical tools for navigating a career change, action steps to get the job you want, and clear guidance in dealing with barriers that get in your way. The next twelve chapters will be broken down into three sections.

Section One: Career Change Kick-Start

We will focus on developing your vision, building the strategy to achieve that vision, and how to access the hidden job market, where most of the opportunities you are looking for probably are.

Section Two: Mastering Your Business Relationships

This section unpacks how to build and nurture better relationships; how to craft your career story; and how to talk, write, and further communicate about your impact to those that will support and hire you.

Section Three: Career Momentum—What Gets in Your Way

Here, we will address the things that get in the way of your progress, how to identify them, and strategies for limiting their impact on your progress and success.

Each section will guide you through understanding the topic, including exercises you can do right now to put into action what you are learning, as well as resources you can download to continue working through the content.

Throughout this section, a few themes will emerge:

- **Actions speak louder than words.**

    We can create the best strategy possible, but without action, that plan is just a piece of paper. You can clearly identify your wants and dreams, but without action, they will remain thoughts in your head, never becoming reality. Action is the secret sauce to your success.

- **Self-understanding leads to better action.**

    The better you know yourself, what you do and don't want, the easier it is to do everything else that follows. Whether designing your strategy, building your action plan, creating a map of your network, or navigating the blocks that get in the way of your progress, the more you engage in the self-discovery process, the better your outcomes will be.

Part Two Introduction

- **Relationships drive everything.**

  Your relationships are the key driver of your career growth. They provide guidance, support, and access to every part of the career growth journey. Without building, nurturing, and supporting those relationships, your career growth opportunities will be limited.

Let's jump in!

Section One:
Career Change Kick-Start

12

WHAT DO YOU WANT?

When it comes to your dreams, you have two choices: pursue them or be haunted by them.

—MEL ROBBINS

An obvious challenge people face is that they don't know what they want. They're far too busy justifying what they think they need. They haven't learned to be brutally honest with themselves and others. They're still living in fear.

—DAN SULLIVAN

Are you burned out? Maybe you are just a little singed?

It's possible that you are living your best life, free from chronic workplace stress and overwhelm due to the ridiculous demands on your time and attention that come from, well, everyone. From your work, your family, your kids, your partner, your culture, the media, fucking Instagram—the systems and structures and people that tell you what to do, how to do it, and that you have to do it all, have it all, be it all.

If you are living your best life, rock and roll! Most of us are not. Most of us are sitting in the car screaming, "Fuck! Make it stop!"

We live in a culture of overwork, competition, and a winner-takes-all mentality, and our workplace cultures reward and promote based on it. There's a lack of workplace support for stressed-out and overworked employees, a lack of adequate parental leave and affordable childcare. There's the impact of the gender pay gap, gender authority gap, gender burnout gap, gender unpaid labor gap. The people and environments that don't give a shit about the gaps are all contributing to the burnout epidemic we are living in. We are fed up, tired of sacrificing our life to the altar of our work. We want something different. We have been trying to do this thing called work–life balance for years, and it isn't working.

We have one life. That's it. How we choose to live that life is all that matters. Your life is the container for everything that weaves in and out of it. Everything else is there to serve that life. And we get to determine what things support that life and what else gets in the way.

Your career, your work, is there to support that life. It has a big role to play because it provides the primary financial contribution, which is wicked important. But it is a slice, not the whole pie. When you approach your career growth through the lens of what you want your life to look like, you will make different choices about what you do, who you do it for, and how much money you need to live.

* * *

To find that next right-fit career step, we first need to figure out

- what you want, or what you don't want (which is sometimes easier to identify);
- what makes *where you are* the wrong fit; and
- how you want your right-fit career to serve the life you want to live.

When was the last time you sat down to ask yourself, *What do I want?* It's probably been a minute. I don't mean what you want for dinner, what kind of vacation to go on, or what you want for your kids or family. Not even what you wanted yesterday, or two, five, or ten years ago. I mean now. What we want is ever-changing, as we are. Our wants in college, the ones that fit us then, are not the same as they are today. What fit you two years ago, one year ago, or six months ago might not fit anymore either.

Choice has been kept from women since, well, forever, and continues to be a matter of debate. This pre-scripting of our identity—controlling what we should or should not do, who we can and cannot be—happens in subtle and not-so-subtle ways. So it is not surprising if no one has asked you what you truly want, or if you have not asked yourself. The idea of actually asking women what they want is a radical idea. Women taking what they want, designing lives on their own terms, and building pathways to get what they truly want is revolutionary.

So why ask? Because if we don't ask ourselves what we want, then who will? It is vital that we make sure we are living lives of our own design, and that we are building a career and spending time in jobs that support those lives.

It is easier to focus on other people's wants and needs, but today we are focusing on you. You are the most important part of this conversation. Let's say that again. You are the most important part of this conversation. I know it feels antithetical to everything you have been taught and feel, but bear with me. I'm not going to give you the whole "put your mask on first before helping others" speech. Even though that is a part of it, and true.

If we are going to find your next right-fit career move, it's time to focus on your needs. You are, after all, the founder and CEO of your family, with the support of your cofounder if you have one of those, but you don't need one. You drive the vision for your family, and they need you to be mentally, physically, and emotionally healthy, as well as happy, engaged, and fulfilled. If you are sacrificing and ignoring yourself, your wants and needs, for the needs of your family, you are making it more difficult for you and your family to thrive. Focusing on you and your needs is good for everyone!

"So, how do I figure out what I want?" you may ask.

Let's find out.

Knowing What You Don't Want

Sometimes knowing what you want can feel overwhelming. Hell, maybe you are just trying to

- get through the day;
- get out of your toxic workplace;
- keep from screaming at the top of your lungs for everyone to get out of your effing way; or
- maybe you just want the space to go to the bathroom in peace, so you can think.

Knowing what you want is crucial because it filters out all of the stuff that gets in the way of your progress. It reduces the stress of indecision so you can focus your attention and achieve your goals with more efficiency and clarity. But guess what. Knowing what you *don't* want does the same thing.

Focusing our attention on what we *don't* want, before we try to figure out what we *do* want, allows us to go into the visioning process free of clutter. It's like cleaning your desk of all the crap before starting work, or organizing your spice cabinet before you go shopping to make that new Latin dish so you don't buy a shit-ton of spices you didn't realize you already have.

Acknowledging your *don'ts* before your *dos* will simplify the visioning process. To do this, grab your notebook, notes app, or the back of a napkin and freewrite all the things you don't want. Just get all that shit out of your brain and onto a piece of paper.

Start by filling in the blanks below:

- I don't want to feel _____.
- I don't want to do _____.
- I don't want to be treated like _____.
- I don't want to be somewhere _____.
- I don't want to be _____.

I'll start. This is what I wrote when I did this exercise before quitting my executive government job a couple years ago:

- I don't want to feel powerless and on edge all the time.
- I don't want to do all this work securing high-profile partnerships that aren't valued.
- I don't want to be treated like my time and attention don't matter.
- I don't want to be somewhere that takes more from my mental and emotional health than it gives back.

- I don't want to be in the same place a year from now, feeling the same way, doing the same thing.

After understanding what I didn't want, my solution was to quit my executive gig and focus on my health and happiness, and launch my business full-time. Here's what that's done for me:

- Reduced my stress and empowered me
- Allowed me to make the most out of my social capital and follow through on the strategic partnerships I develop
- Given me back my time and attention to use as I see fit
- Improved my mental and emotional health
- Allowed me to feel very differently than I did a couple years ago

Now it's your turn. Write down what you don't want.

Once you have finished writing down what you don't want, let's get into discovering what you do want.

Vision Exercise

This three-step exercise will help you understand what you want, prepare you to design an effective strategy and action plan to find that next right-fit career opportunity, and align it with your vision.

Step One: Set Your Intention

When you set an intention, you make a commitment to yourself. Your intention is not set on a specific outcome you have for your life; it is a commitment to the process for developing that vision. Your intention is a powerful tool for clearing your mind and focusing your attention.

Intentions are different from goals. Intentions are about the journey; goals are about the destination. Your intentions focus on your present state of mind and the commitments you make to yourself about reaching your goals. Your goals, on the other hand, focus on the future actions you will take to reach them.

For example, your intention might be to **focus on your breath**, or to **practice patience and grace** with yourself as you go through the visioning process. It might be to **stay positive and limit negative self-talk** so you can write your career story or reach out to some of the people in your network. Writing your intention down every day will help lock it in, make it easier to absorb and connect to. Write it on a sticky note and stick it to your bathroom mirror or in your home-office nook, wherever your glimpse of it will remind you to breathe, practice patience and grace, or stay positive.

Step Two: Remove the Distractions

Distractions come in two broad categories: **internal distractions** and **external distractions**. To tap into your vision, you need to turn them both off.

Internal distractions are all the shit going on inside your head and within your body that keep you from focusing on developing that clear vision. This could be critical self-talk, rumination, or self-doubt, to name a few. It could also be physical manifestations of fear, like a quickening heartbeat or the fight-or-flight response. It is not unusual for visioning work to bump up against some uninvited fear.

When fear pops up, go to your breath, and remember, fear is universal—everyone feels it. Fear rises when we feel some kind of threat, whether physical, mental, or emotional. There is nothing wrong with fear; it is there to help us prepare to deal with some oncoming real or perceived harm. Looking into our wants and needs can make us question what the fuck we are doing, who we are with, and why we have made the choices we have. That can be scary.

Fear may start in our mind but it is felt in our body. It makes us nervous, can cause an upset stomach, affect our sleep, and so much more. The more we hide from or avoid our fears, the longer we sit in the physical and mental impacts of them, and the longer we avoid taking action to reach our goals.

Fear is our friend, not our enemy. It presents a beautiful opportunity to check in on our wants and needs and to better understand what is going on. So give your fear some attention. Sit down with it. Grab a cup of coffee or a cocktail with it, and listen and learn.

Next, work on removing the **external distractions**. Thanks to technology, the needs of family and kids, micromanaging supervisors, and 24/7 accessibility, we deal with a lot of external distractions. Technology distractions are pretty straightforward to turn off. Engage the do-not-disturb or airplane-mode settings, click the little rice-sized switch on the side of your phone till you see orange, and exert your right to say "no" to the ever-expanding notifications. Or just turn off your phone, your watch, and all other devices that talk to you, beep, or otherwise pull your attention during the day.

Turn off the human distractions as well. Since you unfortunately can't press a button to do this, remove yourself from a noisy home or crowded office space. Tell partners or friends to leave you be while you are working on your vision. If you choose to share this work with them, let them know you are not interested in feedback or insight or opinion right now. This is your process, not theirs. Some of what you discover may impact those you love, but right now *you* are your focus. This may seem strange when you have a partner, kids, or family that are intricately tied to your vision, but if you don't remove yourself from them and them from you while you are working on this, it will be difficult to distinguish between what you want because *you* want it and what you want because it's what *everyone else* wants.

Step Three: It's All About the Questions

Visioning is all about the questions. The answers are the icing, but the questions are the cake. Good questions lead you beyond your logical and rational mind and tap into your emotions, senses, and imagination. So embrace the questions and have a little fun.

Let's start with your environment.

Close your eyes and imagine: in your head, just picture the answers to each of the questions below. Turn your phone to do-not-disturb mode. Close the door to your room or the bathroom, or wherever you are. Find a quiet place away from people, and ask yourself:

- Where do *you* want to wake up every morning?
- What do you see out your window in this place?
- What wakes you up?
- How do you feel when you wake up?
- What do you do first thing in the morning?

Remember, focus on you. In this exercise, you are alone. This does not include other people: partners, kids, family, roommates, etc. This is about where *you* want to be. Sink into these questions; enjoy imagining and walking through your senses. Let's continue.

- What can you hear while you drink your coffee, smoothie, or whatever you might be consuming first thing when you wake up? Is the window open? Are you on a balcony or porch or stoop?
- What does it feel like on your skin where you are? Is the air humid, dry, or crisp? What is the season?
- What does it sound like? Can you hear transportation, birds, waves, music from down the way, or conversations in the distance?
- What does it taste like to be where you are? Is it salty, or is it sweet? Is it rich, or is it light?

Next, go back to the top and ask yourself all of the same questions, except this time about where you *currently* live, not where you want to live.

- Where do you *currently* wake up every morning?
- What do you see out your window every day?
- What wakes you up in the morning?
- How do you feel when you wake up in the morning? What do you do first thing in the morning?
- What can you hear while you drink your coffee or smoothie in the morning? Is the window open? Are you on a balcony, a porch, or a stoop?
- What does it feel like on your skin where you live? Is the air humid, dry, or crisp? What is the season?

- What does it sound like? Can you hear transportation, birds, waves, music from down the way, or conversations in the distance?
- What does it taste like to be where you live? Is it salty, or is it sweet? Is it rich, or is it light?

Next, ask yourself these questions:

- How did I get to this place? Was it a choice I made, or was the choice made by someone else? For example, am I living here because it is where I grew up, or did I choose to move here for some reason?
- Did I come here for a job or a person? If so, what was that reason?
- Is the thing or circumstance that brought you here still relevant to your life today?
- What keeps you here? Why do you stay?
- Reflect on the place you are currently living versus the place you want to live. How aligned are they?

After you finish imagining your environment, grab the Vision Exercise resource in the Resources section at the end of the book. It includes the rest of the environmental prompts as well as questions in the following categories:

- People in your life
- Career aspirations and finances
- Health
- Experiences

Allow this process to take some time. Let your imagination wander. Don't rush it. Push away thoughts like *I can't have that* or *that's not reasonable* or *this is weird*. There will be plenty of time to create a practical plan of action to implement your new vision, and yes, it is weird, but do it anyway.

Main Takeaway

The better you understand what *you* want and don't want, independent of what you want for the people you love, the easier it will be to build a life that supports you all. Self-understanding is essential to your success, fulfillment, and happiness at work and in life.

13

THE RIGHT-FIT MATRIX

We have all a better guide in ourselves, if we would attend to it, than any other person can be.

—JANE AUSTEN

In fashion, fit is obvious. Like that pair of soft corduroy pants from the early aughts with the drawstring and huge pockets, buried in the back of my closet. I can step into them and clearly discover they don't fit. Yet there is no model for a right-fit relationship. It is different for everyone. Culture and media may impress upon us that our ideal person should look and behave a certain way, but in reality, we sift through that ideal and make up our own minds.

In general, when we are surrounded by people who encourage, inspire, motivate, and support us, the fit is better than spending time with those who cut us down, judge us, or are unkind and generally behave like assholes. Over time, we get better at identifying the characteristics that complement us and make us feel safe and cared for, and identifying those that don't. We get better at determining what is a good fit.

The right-fit career opportunity is similar. We sift through the pressure to have a certain kind of career, then reflect on the work experience we have already had, in order to find something that provides the support we need to live our lives the way we want to—to find our fit.

The process looks like this:

1. Complete the Visioning Exercise so you have an idea what you want your life to look like, as described in Chapter 12.
2. Assess what has and has not worked in your previous career opportunities through the Career Review. We will get into that in detail below.
3. Align what you learned from the Vision Exercise and the Career Review through the Right-Fit Matrix.

The previous chapter, "What Do You Want?" and the resources that accompany it will help you identify what you want that life to look like. Below, let's unpack the elements included in the Career Review and the Right-Fit Matrix. Worksheets for both will be included in the Resources section at the end of the book.

The Career Review

The past holds your building blocks for the future. Before crafting a strategy for moving forward, let's turn around to take a look behind. A Career Review provides a structured way of processing your career history: what worked, what didn't, and why. Through guided questions, it helps you organize your experience and empower you to make an informed choice about what work adventure to choose next. The questions fall into the following five categories: Arrival, Expectations, Reality, Workplace Culture, and the Future.

Arrival

The Arrival section focuses on how you landed on your previous career or job choice in the first place. Maybe it was passion or obligation, or you may have fallen into your career accidentally. Once you better understand your previous motivation, you can clarify how that aligns with your current one.

Expectations

Our expectations can be a powerful lever of our experience. As author Dr. Elizabeth Scott states, "Expectations refer to the beliefs that you hold about the outcomes of events. While these expectations can play an important role in determining what happens and can contribute to goal-directed behavior, they can also lead to disappointment when reality does not match up to what you had hoped would happen."[25]

Our expectations can drive our feelings of contentment or frustration. They can increase our anxiety when they aren't met and drive us to stay longer in a lousy place or situation as we try to change our reality to match our expectations. By understanding our previous career expectations, we can explore how they may have informed our choice of career up till now.

Reality

Our reality explores the flip side of our expectations and captures what really happened. In this section, we want the truth as you experienced it. Be honest and take your time. Some of this may bring up strong emotions (or not), and that's okay. Whatever you feel and write down is perfectly fine and useful. Judgment is not helpful here; it is a distraction and often a mirror of what *others* believe, not what *you* believe—so leave it outside, and shut the door.

Workplace Culture

Forbes describes workplace culture as the "shared values, belief systems, attitudes and the set of assumptions that people in a workplace share."[26] Workplace culture forms based on consistent

---

25. Elizabeth Scott, "The Expectations vs. Reality Trap," Verywell Mind, updated April 18, 2022, https://www.verywellmind.com/expectation-vs-reality-trap-4570968.

26. Pragya Agarwal, "How to Create a Positive Workplace Culture," *Forbes*, Aug 29, 2018, https://www.forbes.com/sites/pragyaagarwaleurope/2018/08/29/how-to-create-a-positive-work-place-culture/?sh=6e37fd044272.

and reinforced behaviors and interactions between leadership, staff, customers, and work community—and the environment they happen in. According to Indeed, a healthy workplace culture includes accountability, equity, expression, communication, and recognition. The Career Review will ask you to reflect on each of these areas, exploring the following questions:

- How has **accountability** shown up in your workplace—both positively and negatively? Accountability refers to ownership of responsibilities, and trust and transparency about how they are managed and communicated about.
- How was **equity** represented (or not represented) in your workplace regarding hiring, division of workload, and the feeling of being valued and understood?
- How free did/do you feel in your workplace to **express** who you are—your identity, your individuality, your creativity, your expertise, and your experiences?
- How safe and free do you feel to **communicate** your ideas or any challenges you may be having? Are you encouraged to provide and receive feedback and problem-solve with the team?
- **Recognition** can show up in informal and formal praise from leadership, colleagues, or customers, as well as in competitive salaries, and more. How recognized are/were you for your work?

You will discover as you work through these questions that some of the categories are more important to you than others. You may be less interested in being able to express yourself at work, or maybe you don't give a shit about recognition. On the other hand, you might need a work environment that values self-expression and acknowledges its employees regularly for their effort and impact. Don't judge your reaction. Remember, you are performing this audit to find *your* right-fit career opportunity, not someone else's idea of what "right fit" should mean to you.

The Future

Taking into account what you have discovered through each of the previous sections, the next set of questions will focus on what you imagine your *future* career opportunity looks like and how you want it to support you differently than your previous one.

Allow the reflection from the Career Review to empower you to make an informed decision about your next work adventure. It is important to know what you like and dislike, what kind of environment encourages you to do your best work and which does not, and what elements of work culture are the most important for you to thrive. These answers will help you assess your upcoming opportunities so you don't find yourself stuck in the same stressed work environment you just left.

The Right-Fit Matrix

The Right-Fit Matrix is where your Vision Exercise and Career Review overlap. It combines, distills, and summarizes the reflection you have done into four areas.

- **Wants:** Priorities for Career Aspirations and Finances
- **Don't Wants:** Priorities for What You Don't Want
- **Culture:** Workplace Culture Priorities
- **Type:** Work-Type Priorities

The Right-Fit Matrix requires you to make choices about what are the most important elements of your new career aspirations, and what aspects are more agile. For example, whether you work in person, remote, or hybrid may not matter to you. But due to your personal and relational goals, having clearly defined work hours may. Perhaps money is a primary motivator, while recognition and your ability to express yourself are not. You will receive a worksheet in the Resources section to help you with completing your Right-Fit Matrix. In the meantime, let's break down each section.

Wants: Priorities for Career Aspirations and Finances

The Vision Exercise in the Resources section will guide you through the Career Aspirations and Finances section, which focuses on what you want your future career to look like, what you want it to feel like, and how it will support the life you live. It will also help you explore how much money you want to earn in order to make that vision a reality. The Right-Fit Matrix will ask you to condense and then rank your top three priorities from that exercise.

For example, it might look like this:

1. Salary
2. Seniority
3. In-Person Work Location

or

1. Flexibility
2. Predictable Workload
3. Benefit Structure

or

1. Opportunities for Creativity and Innovation
2. Collaborative Work Environment
3. Hybrid Work Location

Don't Wants: Priorities for What you Don't Want

Your Don't Wants are your nonnegotiables: what you will not accept in your career and your life moving forward. It may be a type of work. Maybe you've been in the executive hospitality space, organizing large fund-raising events or executive retreats, but you're tired of being the on-site operations manager. The pace and on-demand nature of event days doesn't fit with your lifestyle anymore, and you are looking for a role that takes advantage of your skills without requiring you to sacrifice control of your time.

You may be unwilling to accept certain behavior in a boss, a level of stress in the workplace, or a salary amount. It is important to know where you are inflexible, and honor that. It will help you identify the red flags or warning signs that a job or workplace is going off the rails toward the unacceptable. Again, the Right-Fit Matrix will ask you to condense and then rank your top three *don't wants*.

Culture: Workplace Culture Priorities

Scan your Career Review Worksheet and identify the top three elements of workplace culture that matter most to you. Be honest with yourself. It is okay if accountability matters less than equity, or if expression is more important to you than recognition. Whatever mash-up works for you is all that matters in this circumstance. Write them down.

Type: Work-Type Priorities

The Career Aspirations and Finances section of the Vision Exercise focuses on the big picture: what you want your career opportunity to look like, what you want it to feel like, and how it supports the life you live. The Work-Type section zooms in and focuses specifically on what you want to *do*. For example, you might be looking for a managerial position, or to get *out* of a management position. It could be that you are seeking more leadership opportunities and to move away from project management. You may want a hybrid or fully remote position, or the possibility of travel. Perhaps you are eager to find a position that will take advantage of your language skills and situate you as an asset in the company's work globally. Whatever your top three work-type priorities are, write them down.

As you complete the Right-Fit Matrix, you will notice that some of the priorities in each of the four areas will overlap, which indicates their increased value. No career move will be perfect, but knowing your priorities will help you vet opportunities, ask better questions, and avoid making a career move that negatively impacts your well-being. It will help keep you from returning to a work type, roles and responsibilities, leaders and team environments, or a workplace culture where you can't do your best work.

13

Main Takeaway

It's hard to know where to go if you don't know where you have been. Your vision paints the picture of your future. Your Career Review reflects upon your past. The Right-Fit Matrix fuses the two into a guide you can use in the present to find your next right-fit career opportunity.

14

YOUR CAREER GROWTH STRATEGY

You do not rise to the level of your goals. You fall to the level of your systems. Your goal is your desired outcome. Your system is the collection of daily habits that will get you there.

—JAMES CLEAR

Now that you better understand what you want for your life, have unpacked your past career experience, and identified how your new work will support you differently moving forward, it is time to develop your strategy.

Your right-fit career strategy is the plan and actions that will lead you to your right-fit career. It protects your time and resources and assures that your actions lead directly to your goals. Without a strategy, you are taking action without any aim. A strategy saves you from the more-is-better approach, which has you endlessly applying to job postings without the support of your network, hoping someone will notice your effort and offer you a new opportunity, or attending more events out of obligation, not knowing how they help you reach your goals.

Why You Need a Strategy

There are three reasons you need a right-fit career strategy:

1. **So you don't have to wake up every day and wonder what to do.**

    Your Strategy tells you what to do so you can take action confidently and quickly and then move on to what you need to do next. It removes the decision fatigue of not knowing what actions to take, when, and how. Too much time is wasted in inaction, indecision, thinking about what to do, and wavering back and forth. Your strategy will outline what to do so all you have to do is take the actions identified for that part of the strategy.

2. **To hold you accountable to your goals.**

    Personal accountability creates reliability and trust in yourself. Your strategy is like your inanimate accountability partner. When you are accountable, you are willing to accept responsibility for your choices, actions, and inactions. It can be hard to hold yourself responsible when you don't know what to do next, but it is essential, and your strategy gives you the path to follow. It reminds you of the things that need to be done when you haven't done them. It says, "Come on, let's get going; you have things to do to build your dream career opportunities."

3. To track your progress.

Tracking your progress allows you to see how much you have accomplished! Finding your next right-fit career opportunity and building the relationships that will get you there can be a long game. Sometimes it is hard to see your progress when you are working your plan, taking action, having conversations, and attending events. But by logging the actions you take, writing down the people you connect with, and taking notes on your discussions, you can follow up more quickly, nurture those conversations, and send them updates or articles related to what you discussed. All this puts your progress in perspective, even when it may not feel like you are moving as fast as you want to.

Your Strategy is broken down into three sections:

- Intention/Purpose—why you want what you want
- Actions—what you are going to do
- Tracking—how you know you've done it

Let's dig into each one.

Strategy Section One: Intention/Purpose—Why You Want What You Want

As we touched on in depth in Chapter 12, knowing what you want is a powerful tool for focusing your attention. Perhaps you want to come back to work after a career break, or you're looking for a job in a new industry or seeking a promotion. Maybe you want to be appointed to a certain committee that will help advance your career. You might be tired of the pressure to ascend to the C-suite and want to make a lateral move that retains your seniority, reduces the amount of people you manage, and provides more flexibility.

It is essential to know what you want. But to what end? What is the purpose of those interests? Your purpose illustrates why those wants matter. It keeps you focused on the big picture, brings you back to center if you get derailed or distracted, and gives you a rubric to measure your actions against to keep you on track.

Here are a few examples:

1. WANT: You might be coming off a career break and are eager to find a career opportunity that takes into account your previous expertise without penalizing you for the time away.

WHY: Maybe you took a break to focus on raising your kids full-time. You have loved that time with them, but if you have to be home any longer, you might scream. You feel yourself getting lost as a stay-at-home parent. You spent years building your expertise before kids, and you take pride in using those skills to help your employer succeed. You want to feel that again, and you miss the challenge and camaraderie of work. The regular non-kid-related adult interaction would also be great.

2. WANT: You might want to leave your current industry for a new one.

WHY: Perhaps you are exhausted from the lack of support you receive as an associate professor and manager in higher education. The work has been interesting, but with all the budget challenges, your dean and chair dumping excessive work in your lap, and the workplace politics, you are burned out and ready for a change. You want to find work in an industry you are more passionate about, and a job that pays more so you can explore new areas of interest and travel.

3. WANT: Maybe you enjoy the industry you are in, but you want to shift your managerial responsibilities without losing seniority.

WHY: Let's imagine you have spent the past ten years striving for a C-suite position because you are ambitious and that is what you are supposed to do when you are a goal-getter. But as you rise in the ranks, the work gets less interesting and requires more time on activities you really dislike. You've discovered that managing people is not your jam, and most of the women you know in the C-suite are miserable. So you want to shift gears, manage fewer people, and create more time in your schedule to figure out a new long-term path for your career that saves you from the misery you see around you.

4. WANT: You manage a team in a large company and want to switch divisions because the vice president you report to behaves like an asshole and there is no room for growth.

WHY: You don't enjoy going to work, and the best days are when your VP is out of the office traveling. You know you have more to give, but the work culture is impacting the quality of your work and the work of those you manage. You do your best to protect your direct reports from interaction with the VP, but his overly critical and sometimes inappropriate or volatile behavior is unacceptable and impacting your mental and emotional health. You are committed to the company and what it stands for, and you are eager to grow your career within it, but working in this division makes that impossible.

14

Strategy Section Two: Actions—What You Are Going to Do

Now that you have identified the *why* behind your wants, it's time to do something about it. The next step is to break your wants into actions and build those actions into habits. Due in part to my appreciation of the habit master (James Clear) and my action-obsessed upbringing (thanks, Mom and Dad), I prefer sliding over goals altogether and going straight to actions. Goals can add an unnecessary administrative step between understanding what you want and taking the actions to achieve it.

Your actions determine your outcome. You can't think or plan your way into your right-fit career. You must act. Some of your actions will be singular; most of them will create habits, which are the collection of actions that repeat over and over again. These habits build the practice that leads you to achieving what you've outlined in your strategy. Whether it's relationship-building, career research, or self-promotion, repetition is the key.

We confirm our priorities through our actions. Perhaps we want to reduce stress, learn a new language, or read more books. If we keep hanging out with the people who stress us out the most, never download Duolingo, or spend all our downtime watching Netflix, how devoted are we to those goals? We can say we are desperate for a career change, but if we never take action to explore it, how committed are we to that change? Our actions betray our commitment and cast a shadow over our words if they are out of sync.

The Risk of Inaction

We often think of risk in terms of the actions we take. But there is an even bigger risk, and that is the risk of doing nothing—the risk of *not* taking action. There is a potential cost associated with the actions we take and the actions we don't take. We are often hyperaware of the cost of action but don't consider the cost of inaction. If there is a gap between where you are and where you want to be, not taking action costs you dearly.

If you are unsatisfied with your work:

- it costs you the physical, mental, and emotional stress of burnout;
- it costs you in unearned salary or revenue; and
- it costs you in leadership opportunities and the benefits of being challenged and finding meaning and belonging through your work.

If you are unsatisfied with your life:

- it costs you the time and attention you are not spending on your personal relationships; and
- it costs you the mental, emotional, and physical stress that comes along with not living the life you want.

Reducing Self-Sabotage

Sometimes fear of the unknown, uncertainty, and discomfort take hold and lead us into self-sabotaging behaviors that keep us from taking action. Here are seven questions you can ask yourself to get at the root of your fear, stop your self-sabotaging behaviors, and start taking action now!

1. **What is your self-sabotaging behavior?**

    Take a look at your behaviors. See if you can identify the ones that are getting in the way of you meeting your goals, and ask trusted friends for help if you need to. If you are still having trouble identifying the behaviors that stall your forward momentum, spend a week tracking your time. Sometimes we fill our days with extra stuff in order to avoid taking action on the things we say we want to do. You will receive access to a worksheet to help you do this in the Resources section at the end of the book.

2. **What would happen if you stopped that behavior?**

    Imagine what is possible, what you could accomplish, where you could go, who you could be, and who you could help if you stopped that behavior.

3. **Why are you avoiding [insert the thing that would happen if you stopped the behavior]?**

    What do you gain by avoiding that thing? You must be getting something out of it. Does it alleviate some external or internal pressure? Does it keep you or other people in your life more comfortable? Sometimes we avoid taking action because we are spending too much time managing other people's expectations or emotions instead of focusing on our own dreams.

4. **What is the worst thing that could happen if you do the thing you are avoiding?**
   Is there a consequence to doing what you are avoiding? Project into the future and imagine the worst outcome. What do you lose? How are you or others harmed?

5. **Can you handle it if that worst thing happens?**
   On the scale of totally manageable, I can handle it, to hello no, I can't handle it, where does it fall?

6. **What will happen if you continue the self-sabotaging behavior and never accomplish [insert the thing that would happen if you stopped the behavior]?**
   Clearly identify what will happen if you continue to choose inaction.

7. **What will you do?**
   After going through the first six questions, ask yourself to actively choose what direction to take. Will you continue your self-sabotaging behavior, or will you stop, change course, and take action?

How the Actions Look in Your Strategy

The actions in your strategy will break down into **primary, secondary,** and **additional actions.** Let's take a look at how to deconstruct wants into these actions.

Let's go back to the supervisor example from above, the VP who has been behaving like an asshole:

WANT: You manage a team in a large company and want to switch divisions because the vice president you report to behaves like an asshole.

WHY: You don't enjoy going to work, and the best days are when your VP is out of the office traveling. You know you have more to give, but the work culture is impacting the quality of your work and the work of those you manage. You do your best to protect your direct reports from interaction with the VP, but his overly critical and sometimes inappropriate or volatile behavior is unacceptable and impacting your mental and emotional health. You are committed to the company and what it stands for, and you are eager to grow your career within it, but working in this division makes that impossible.

From the description above, clearly the fit is off. What you WANT is:

- to remain in your company if possible;
- to be in a division led by a supportive VP who creates a safe and productive environment for you and your team to do your best work; and
- to be challenged at work with opportunities for growth.

To achieve this, you can start by taking these first three primary actions and the secondary action steps that follow.

Primary Action One

Research your current company to see what opportunities might already exist internally to move from the division you are in.

This singular action can be broken down into three **secondary action** steps:

1. Read through company-wide newsletters or communications, looking for information on expansion or creation of new teams. Is the company developing any new committees that might connect you with different leaders or collaborators?
2. Take a look at the organizational chart for your company so you understand who does what and reports to whom. Identify what executive staff hiring, firing, or shuffling is happening. This will tell you which teams are in flux.
3. Google-stalk your company to find out how the company, or its products and services, are being talked about in the news. Is the press bad or good? Is it about expansion, or contraction? How is work culture discussed? What are peers and competitors saying publicly?

Knowledge is power, and each of these three secondary actions will lead you to additional actions. They will illuminate potential opportunities in your company and who to talk to about them. You can do the same primary and secondary actions to explore opportunities in your peer and competing companies if you are unable to make an internal shift.

Primary Action Two

Raise your profile and build your thought leadership, engage in conversation with peers and leaders in your company, and keep up with other thought leaders in your industry. This can be broken down into the following **secondary action** steps

1. Write your career story. The better you understand your impact, the easier it will be to find subjects to discuss that take advantage of your unique skills and expertise. **Additional actions** might be to break down your work so far into quantitative and qualitative metrics so you have a clear understanding of your impact. Find someone to help you with this if you find it difficult.
2. Update your LinkedIn profile to reflect your career story and the impact you deliver. Focus the language on where you want to go and not just where you have been. **Additional actions** would be to start posting consistently on LinkedIn, connect with thought leaders in your industry, and engage regularly with their content.
3. Identify new opportunities to speak or provide your insight and expertise. This could be giving presentations within or outside your company. Or it could mean participating in company-wide or industry-wide

committees or groups that are established to solve challenges. **Additional actions** could be to talk with any managers responsible for professional development, offering to do a training on something you are passionate about, or identify who plans your industry conference and offer to contribute to a panel.

Your strategy is a living document that strengthens and grows the more you use it. Each of the primary, secondary, and additional actions will lead to more action steps to take. You will subscribe to industry news publications, discover industry associations you can be a part of, identify industry leaders to connect with, find new ways to talk about your impact, and so much more. As your action list grows, you will discover new pockets of opportunity and connect with the people who manage those options.

Strategy Section Three: Tracking—How You Know You've Done It

Your strategy provides you with the roadmap to your right-fit career. By following it, you will discover the new opportunities you seek. Some of this will happen quickly, and a lot of it will develop over time. Tracking your progress helps you monitor what you have to do next and showcases all you have accomplished so far. As you take each action step, check off the item and celebrate the little wins along the way. Progress comes from the commitment to taking consistent action daily, so track your actions religiously, and watch as you move closer to your career growth goals.

Make sure you track the following things:

1. The **completion** of all primary, secondary, and additional actions you have added to your list. Check them off.
2. The **addition** of all new action items. Write down any new actions that you add to your list. It might seem tedious, but I promise you it will feel good to look at the progress you are making with all the actions you are taking.
3. The **people** you are connecting with. These are people you reach out to and people who reach out to you. Keep track of your history of reaching out when you connected, highlights of your conversations/ communication, and next steps/follow-up actions. We will talk more about this in the next section.

Flip the page, and let's get into it.

Main Takeaway

Your commitment to taking action is your pathway to finding that next right-fit opportunity. Without action, your wants remain figments of your imagination instead of your reality.

15

THE HIDDEN JOB MARKET

As an actor, what's interesting is what's hidden away beneath the surface. You want to be like a duck on a pond—very calm on the surface but paddling away like crazy underneath.

—ALEXANDER SKARSGÅRD

Suppose you are spending your time rewriting your résumé for the hundredth time and only applying to posted job opportunities. In that case, you are following a *reactive* career growth strategy: "acting in response to a situation rather than creating or controlling it," as Oxford Languages describes it.

A *proactive* strategy focuses on identifying the challenges and problems that your skills and expertise are uniquely suited to solve, then matching them with the industry or company that is desperate for the solution. It works with company leaders, hiring managers, and your business relationships to identify existing and available opportunities and/or create new ones. It relies on creativity, engages your curiosity, and leverages your specific expertise to access both the visible and hidden job market.

A proactive career growth strategy is solution-oriented and requires you to understand your unique value, communicate about it, and listen and learn what is happening in your industry. It asks you to prioritize

- relationship-building over applicant tracking systems;
- industry investigation over keyword research; and
- communicating about *your* value and impact, not your résumé.

The Hidden Job Market—What the Hell Is It?

The hidden job market refers to jobs that are not advertised publicly. Research suggests that 70 to 80 percent of the opportunities are in the hidden job market. "Whether or not this is accurate, two things are certain: There are plenty of job openings that are never publicized, and job seekers who ignore them limit their chances of employment."[27] These jobs tend to be higher-level

---

27. John Feldmann, "Job Seekers: Four Reasons to Embrace the Hidden Job Market," *Forbes*, Mar 21, 2023, https://www.forbes.com/sites/forbeshumanresourcescouncil/2023/03/21/job-seekers-four-reasons-to-embrace-the-hidden-job-market/?sh=52bae0dd6a65.

roles that require unique expertise or special skills. This includes existing positions companies fill internally or externally, positions they haven't yet created, and consulting work necessary to support acute challenges a company may be facing. When hiring for these opportunities, leaders will look internally—within the existing pool of people in the company—and externally, through referrals from employees, colleagues, or friends.

Aside from the casting assistant job in my early twenties, and my entrepreneurial endeavors, the rest of my career opportunities have come from within the hidden job market. In some cases, roles were created for me to build or launch something. Alternatively, I've pitched an employer to bring me in as a consultant to solve a problem they were struggling with. At other times, we have worked together to adapt an existing role into an expanded one that would increase my responsibility. There is more flexibility than you think in your job opportunities.

It's possible the opportunity you are looking for might be within your current company. It benefits your employer in cost per hire and in better retention to hire from within. According to research from the Wharton School of the University of Pennsylvania, it costs your employer 18 percent less to hire from within, 21 percent of external hires are more apt to leave during the first year, and employees stay 41 percent longer at companies that have a history of promoting/hiring from within.[28] Those jobs

---

28. Staff, "Why External Hires Get Paid More, and Perform Worse, than Internal Staff," *Knowledge at Wharton*, March 28, 2012, https://knowledge.wharton.upenn.edu/article/why-external-hires-get-paid-more-and-perform-worse-than-internal-staff/.

may or may not be posted publicly, but even if they are, the qualified internal candidate is far more likely to sail through the hiring/promotion process and get hired.

As discussed earlier, companies will often have acute challenges that require skills or personnel that don't exist on their current roster or don't require a full-time position to be established at the time. They may need to launch a new program, develop new partnerships, review or create new systems, or audit and build in new efficiencies. These opportunities can certainly turn into full-time positions even if they don't start that way, as evidenced by my career trajectory.

Companies may also need someone to serve in a fractional capacity, like a fractional chief financial officer, chief operating officer, or chief marketing officer. These positions provide specialized executive and/or management services on a part-time basis. Someone might work as a fractional CFO at multiple organizations. This might work well for those who are interested in more flexibility and/or less engagement in the company workplace culture, while still earning a competitive salary.

There are multiple kinds of career opportunities within the hidden job market. Whether those jobs are filled internally or an external candidate is brought in, it's crucial to gain an understanding of your industry and the challenges companies face, and to foster your business relationships that bring those opportunities to life.

The Traditional/Visible Job Market Kind of Sucks

The traditional/visible job market kind of sucks. It is not as transparent as it appears to be, as *Forbes* reported in late 2023: "Clarify Capital surveyed 1000 hiring managers in October of 2023 and discovered that 50% of hiring managers created job openings to keep a warm talent pool 'at the ready' for when they are hiring without the intention to hire. This is one of the reasons why job seekers are finding it difficult to navigate the job boards, trying to assess postings that are for real jobs and ones that aren't."[29]

Sometimes, to comply with legal requirements, companies may post jobs they have already informally filled. Two of my former jobs that transitioned from consulting work to full-time positions worked that way. Candidates went through a ghost submission and interview process but were ultimately declined as I was already promised the job.

The traditional job market also relies too heavily on the résumé as a first impression. If hiring managers only spend those six to seven seconds looking at your career history, it leaves little room for nuance, creating another barrier of entry, and reduces a candidacy to keywords.

---

29. Kara Dennison, "How Ghost Job Postings Are Creating a False Sense of Hope," *Forbes*, November 27, 2023, https://www.forbes.com/sites/karadennison/2023/11/27/how-ghost-job-postings-are-creating-a-false-sense-of-hope/?sh=5f6fa92e7dc0.

In the visible job market, all the control sits with the algorithms and hiring managers. Candidates think, *Of course it does; they are the ones doing the hiring! Doesn't it have to? What control do I have?* In general, we often have less control than we think we do but more control than we use. With a proactive approach to your career growth, you exert the control you do have, and unlock more opportunity.

Four Keys to Accessing the Hidden Job Market

Think Like an Entrepreneur

Entrepreneurship is a way of thinking as much as a way of doing business. You don't have to launch a business to take advantage of this perspective. A solution-oriented approach, out-of-the-box thinking, an agile and curious mind, and a resilient nature will set you up to find opportunities in the hidden job market. That interest in understanding how things work, the ability to identify the problems, and collaboratively or individually create solutions is far more valuable to your employer at every level of employment.

An entrepreneurial mindset will also protect you from fluctuations in the job market. Stop obsessing over the job projections, expected layoffs (or not), hiring slowing down (or not)—all it does is stress you out. If you are an out-of-the-box thinker, you will be able to look past the projections to see the opportunity that exists inside change.

Stop Postponing Networking

You keep saying you need to do it, yet you aren't. Why is that? We indicate our priorities by where we allocate our time and attention. What is your time and attention telling you that you value?

Part of the beauty of engaging with your business network are the observations, suggestions, and introductions that open your mind and open doors to career paths you never thought to go down. An agile and open mind creates space for those ideas to be planted, and one of those seeds might become the perfect opportunity.

Let's put it this way: as discussed, research suggests 70 to 80 percent of jobs are not advertised publicly and roughly 80 percent of jobs are secured through prior relationships. If this is true, and you are not building relationships, you only see 30 percent of the opportunities and are gambling with only a 20 percent chance of securing a spot. We will discuss more specifically how to master your business networking in the next chapter, but it can't be stated enough that your ability to build and nurture relationships is a crucial driver to accessing the hidden job market.

Start Close to Home

The work environments closest to you are your best first options for accessing the hidden job market. Look to your current company before seeking opportunities outside. Notice what is happening: Are teams expanding or contracting? Has a new vice president been given a directive to solve a specific problem? Are there interdepartmental committees being created to address something company-wide?

The more you know about the environment you are working in, where you already have established relationships and common ground, the easier it can be to identify where new opportunities may be bubbling up.

The more you get used to identifying how work environments are shifting, changing, growing, or shrinking, the easier it will be to start noticing opportunities float to the surface. You can pitch yourself for a job already created but not advertised publicly, or collaborate with your employer to create a new one.

Understand Yourself

You are your most important asset, and the better you understand yourself and your unique skills, the easier it is to position yourself as the best candidate for any opportunity in the hidden job market. Your relationships can open doors, but you walk through them. Communicating what you do, the impact you deliver, and why it matters keeps you in the room.

To match your skills and expertise with the challenges your industry or company is facing, you must understand what you bring to the table that might be missing. It could be your perspective or your ability to get the best work out of a team. You could be an expert at refining systems and can identify and remove bottlenecks like no one else. Maybe launching new programs is your specialty. Whatever it is, communicating about it is vital to accessing the hidden job market.

Main Takeaway

You will find more opportunity and have more control over your career growth journey by following a proactive strategy and prioritizing the hidden job market over the traditional/visible market.

Section Two:
Mastering Your Business Relationships

16

WHO'S IN YOUR CIRCLE?

Instead of drifting along like a leaf in a river, understand who you are and how you come across to people and what kind of an impact you have on the people around you and the community around you and the world, so that when you go out, you can feel you have made a positive difference.

—JANE FONDA

It is almost impossible to navigate your career growth without a supportive and engaged business network—people you know, like, and trust, and those who care about you and your personal and professional growth.

Some question how accurate the common statistic is that states roughly 80 percent of jobs are secured through networking. But no matter how "networking" is defined for that statistic, in more cases than not, your business relationships are your access to opportunity; they are the collection of people who will inform, introduce, connect, and hire you for your next job.

You can spend time applying to another eight hundred job postings and let the applicant tracking systems sort you based on keywords. You might get a hiring manager to spend six to seven seconds looking at your résumé, which, according to Indeed, is the average time someone spends reviewing it. You may get a call, an interview, and even be hired, but the investment of time and effort to get you there is out of whack with the number of offers you receive. By reprioritizing a portion of that time to building and nurturing your relationships, you will see your opportunity expand.

When beginning to network, often we discount all the people we already know. We rush out and start connecting to a slew of new people before thinking about who, why, and specifically what we want to talk to those people about. We think we must start over, but you aren't starting over. You are building upon the rich experiences and relationships that have been weaving in and out of your life for years. Those past professional and personal experiences and the relationships we develop from them form the foundation of the support system we need to build our future.

Our Current Relationships

The people we surround ourselves with have the power to impact how we feel and what we do—more power than we want to believe. If we have negative or fearful influences in our corner, what we think is possible for our life will be limited by their point of view. When we spend time with encouraging, out-of-the-box thinkers, we will be more open to the opportunities around us.

Building a supportive community takes intention and action. We have the power to build our community in a way that supports our growth, challenges us to do new things, and energizes us. For some of us, our community may naturally support our dreams and desire for change, but if it does not, we need to do something about that. Too often, we can settle into a community or relationships that don't want us to change. We surround ourselves with people who would prefer we remain in a way that makes *them* the most comfortable and reflects what *they* want us to be, which is not reflective of our dreams and aspirations. This can have a deep impact on what we feel is possible for our life, and influence the actions we take to change it.

The key to building a supportive community is to

1. **audit** the one you have;
2. take control and **design** the community you want; and
3. **nurture** the relationships that you build (we will talk more about the nurturing later, but for now let's dig into the first two).

How to Audit Your Community

Think about the people in your life in concentric circles, with you standing in the center. The first circle includes the people closest to you. All of these people have the most significant impact on you due to their physical proximity or the emotional connection you have with them. They can impact you without much effort due to that closeness. They might be your loved ones, best friends, immediate family, coworkers, or the barista you talk to twice daily due to your latte addiction. A kind word, negative energy, their belief and encouragement, or disdain or criticism can propel or derail your mood, thought patterns, and actions more easily than we would like to admit.

The next circle is a little wider, slightly distant from you. It may take them a couple of steps to reach you. These may include other friends with whom you share a common affinity but aren't as close with or other colleagues you see less often. The emotional connection might be there, but the physical proximity is less, or vice versa. As the circles get wider and wider, those people occupying each circle have less and less access to you. The impact of their presence, words, and actions is limited due to their distance—whether physical, mental, or emotional.

The people in the first couple of circles are influential. Their attitude, support, or feedback can help you or hurt you. Therefore, choosing who you want to be in those powerful positions is essential. You can demote or promote whomever you want, even banish those who are not an abundant or supportive force. You are not obligated to take anyone's bad attitude, lack of support, or shitty behavior just because they have held a spot in one of the inner circles. Plenty of other people—old friends, new friends, colleagues, and peers—will support you. Find them!

Community Audit Exercise

Let's do a little exercise to audit your community. The Resources section at the end of the book will have a worksheet for this exercise as well, but let's do this together right now:

- **Grab a piece of paper. On the top, write Circle One and Circle Two and write down the twentyish people you spend the most time around.**

  These are the people in the first couple of circles. They will be friends, family members, partners, kids, or coworkers, or it could be someone you are on the same schedule with and walk with to get lunch every day. These are not the people you *want* to be around but the people you *actually* spend time with. Whoever they are, write them down.

- **Next, underline everyone on that list who stresses you out, is overly critical, exhausts you to spend time with, or has a negative vibe.**

  We all vent and complain to our friends sometimes, but these are people who constantly complain, bitch about their partner *all* the time, or only talk about how terrible parenting and their kids are. They might talk about things they want to do but never actually do them and always have excuses for not trying, or they believe the world is against them. Watch for funny people who use humor to mask negativity—it is still negativity. You don't need that energy in your life. Underline these people.

No one is going to see this list, so be honest. If you underline your partner, kids, or mom, it is okay. It is essential to know these things. It doesn't mean you are going to dump your partner, ship the kids to live with their aunt, or never see your mom again. Just be honest and underline them.

- **On the top of a separate piece of paper, write Circle Three+ and write down twentyish people you know but *don't* spend much time around.**

These are people who light you up, encourage you, have an abundance mindset, and are doing things you want to be doing, people you feel good being around and talking to but don't see or engage with very often. Write them all down! When you get off a call with these people, you feel better, like the world is more exciting, and full of possibilities.

Now, let's take control of your community based on what you have indicated on your pages.

- Grab the Circle One and Two paper. On the back of the paper, rewrite everyone you underlined.

- Next to each person you rewrote, tag them as Remove, Demote, or Improve.

Remove means they are a negative influence; you don't *have* to spend time with them or don't *want* to spend time with them. You have the power to remove these individuals from your orbit, to make room for other influences, and you can stop spending regular time with them.

Those you **Demote** are people you may still need to see now and then, like the PTA moms who are judgy, those work colleagues, and Uncle Bobby, but you don't have to see them as often. You can skip happy hours with those colleagues, make sure you don't spend one-on-one time with Bobby at family gatherings, and sit with different people at the PTA meeting. Tag these people with **Demote**.

Tag the people that are important enough in your life that you want to improve your relationships with **Improve**. These could be your partner, mom, kids, or other colleagues. Talk to your partner about how you would like to improve your relationship, find different things to discuss with your mom, and develop ways to help your kids explore a more growth-oriented mindset, or find ways you can split the load with your partner, family, or friends.

- **Now look at the Circle Three+ paper. These are the people you don't spend much time around but who are a positive, energizing, and motivating influence in your life. Underline anyone you want to Promote!**

    Promoting them means you want to make an effort to spend more time with them. That might be reaching out more, being in contact via text or DM, or grabbing coffee or lunch if they are local. These are the individuals whose presence, energy, and influence you would love to have more of in your life.

As you do this exercise, you will start noticing the people in your life who are supportive, encouraging, and creative thinkers, and those that are not. You will **Promote** or **Improve** based on what role you want them to play in your life. You will also **Remove** or **Demote** those whose influence discourages your personal and professional growth, and start reconnecting with previous connections and making new ones to fill in the gaps.

Audit Your Digital Community

Your digital community is as powerful as your in-real-life (IRL) community. You are connected to a vast world of other people through social media and other online communities. Whether on LinkedIn, Instagram, TikTok, Facebook, or YouTube, there are a plethora of people who like, follow, and comment on your content who range from "interested in you" to "raving fans."

They may be people you know from high school, college, past jobs, faith communities, personal or professional development activities, or online identity-based groups, to name a few. These are the groups of people you are tangentially connected with based on those shared interests and experiences. This community is a beautiful pool of people within which you can all support, encourage, and help each other reach goals. They should be kind people who influence your life in a positive or growth-oriented way. If they are not, they should not be in your community.

Do the Community Audit exercise for your digital environment, which includes the groups mentioned above and any that exist primarily online. Audit the content you consume and the platforms you spend time on, and make sure you spend time with digital accounts supporting your goals. Perform the Remove, Demote, Improve, or Promote exercise, and unfollow/block the accounts that make you feel bad about yourself, are full of negativity, and don't support who you are and what you want.

Main Takeaway

Don't underestimate the power of the people around you to impact how you feel, what you think is possible for your future, and the action you take to achieve it. Use your power to design the support system you need to make your vision a reality.

17

BUILDING AND NURTURING YOUR RELATIONSHIPS

In my experience, people generally network with people who think, act, and speak just like they do, and then therefore, they never get the benefit of networking with people who have been extremely successful or who have a broader or more worldly point of view.

—MIKE GARGANO

Now that you have audited your in-real-life and digital community and decided what kind of access you want them to have, it's time to start building and nurturing your relationships. When we begin networking, we often get overwhelmed thinking about all the new people we have to contact—yes, you will do some of that. But you will be surprised how many people you already know that can be a supportive influence in your life.

The first and most essential part of building your business relationships is to reconnect with people from past jobs, old college friends, that book club group, and the "new moms" group you loved back in the day. Reach out to everyone you can think of and say hi. I can't emphasize this enough! Before registering for that networking event or signing up for another women's networking community, start talking to people you haven't spoken to in a while. Don't make it more complicated than it needs to be.

Don't worry about what to say or the awkwardness of not having talked for years. It might feel weird, but so what? Do it anyway.

Let's be honest: if you want growth, staying comfortable isn't going to get it done. What's wrong with a bit of discomfort and weirdness now and then? Embrace it. Own it. What's the worst thing that can happen? Someone ghosts you. Another responds, "WTF are you doing reaching out to me? Leave me alone!" Can you survive either of those situations? Of course, you can!

You don't need an extensive network to reap the benefits of networking. In this case, bigger isn't better. A small, robust, engaged network is better than a vast network of people you barely know. More contacts and connections do not lead to a better, stronger, or more supportive network. It just leads to larger numbers and vanity metrics that don't reach out to you with an opportunity or send you an article they thought might help you. Metrics don't do these things; people do—people who know you, like you, and are invested in you and your future.

As we've already discussed, a good relationship allows you to be yourself and includes trust, respect, and open and honest conversation—and it is also reciprocal. You know that person you dated who said they didn't want a "serious" relationship. The one who was never really interested in getting to know you and only reached out with a "what's up" text when they needed something or were lonely? I know you know who I'm talking about. Picture them in your head. How did that relationship make you feel? Maybe the first time they reached out, you felt wanted or needed. It might have been nice to banter back and forth for a minute, but when they asked you to hook up or hook them up, it felt pretty shitty. Your business or personal relationships should not feel like that.

When you reach out to people simply because you want them to do something for you, it feels crappy because it is. You don't know them; they don't know you. Why would they put their reputation on the line and spend their valuable time and energy on that interaction? Why would you?

After building relationships and partnerships for twenty-plus years, I've learned to filter my relationship-building through a rubric of **interest**, **care**, and **energy**. I ask myself these questions:

- Am I *interested* in this person, who they are, and what they do, and are they interested in me? Is it thought-provoking or captivating when I talk to them or hear them speak? Does it pique my curiosity? Do we have something to talk about? Whether for two minutes or two hours, are they focused and attentive to our conversation?
- Do they *care*? While interest and care can overlap, they are also distinct. Where interest is more intellectual and brain-based, care is heart-centered and more focused on emotion. How we treat, value, and care for other people, and how they treat, value, and care for us in return will draw me toward some people and away from others, no matter how we might be able to support each other's growth.
- There isn't a formula for finding the right *energy* or *vibe* with someone. Chris Low is the "head of vibe" at Canva, but according to a *Guardian* article, Canva hasn't defined what "the vibe" is. Here's what Low says: "To box it, to draw lines around it, I don't think is really conducive. We facilitate and allow it to grow naturally."[30] We may not have a clear definition for the *energy* or *vibe*

---

30. Naaman Zhou, "Vibe check: what does the most overused word of our era actually mean?", *Guardian*, March 22, 2023, https://www.theguardian.com/lifeandstyle/2023/mar/22/vibes-definition-slang-language-meaning.

we're seeking, but we will know it when we feel it—and when we don't. Wherever you're networking, look for good vibes, positive interaction, and a little spark. You want to feel a mutual energy connection when getting to know each other. You can undoubtedly network with people you don't vibe with, but it is harder to maintain those relationships in the long term.

You will develop more authentic relationships by looking at networking through a lens of care, interest, and energy. It is not about becoming everyone's best friend; however, you will develop lifelong friends with some of those in your network. It is about creating the kind of business relationships you are eager to connect with—people who are interested in your progress and who you are happy to support as well. It is hard to support people you don't have a genuine interest in and who don't have a genuine interest in you and your goals. Interest, care, and energy are elements that keep networking from feeling scummy and inauthentic. You want to learn who they are, not just what they do and how you think they can help you.

The Four Types of People You Need in Your Network

Before we talk about the four types of people you need in your network, there is one group of people you don't need in your network: people who behave like assholes. That seems obvious, but you would be surprised how much we tolerate bad behavior from the people around us because we think (or they think) they have an important job. There is no "have to" in networking. You do not have to engage with people whose bad behavior is inappropriate or makes you feel uncomfortable. Spending your energy and time on them only hurts your progress, so it bears mentioning.

Here are the four groups of people you *do* need in your network:

1. People on a professional or personal-growth path similar to yours

It is helpful to surround yourself with people who understand the path you are on because, well, they are on it too. It is a relief to have people who get it, so you don't have to explain what you want, or express your goals and what you are doing to achieve them.

If you are looking for that dream job, you want other people around you who know they are meant for more and are tired of settling for a career that doesn't feel right. These people are motivated like you are, searching for something better and looking to improve themselves. They care about their personal and professional development and take a vested interest in yours.

We are sponges, whether we like it or not; our environment and the people in it have a significant impact. If we surround ourselves with people who are afraid of change, primarily negative or critical about what we say or want to do, it increases our fear, encourages us to focus on the worst outcome, and is demotivating. So make sure you have people in your network who are on the same professional or personal growth path as you.

2. People who have work lives like the one you aspire to have

As civil rights activist Marian Wright Edelman said, "You can't be what you can't see."[31] Surrounding yourself with people who have the career life you want to have will challenge you to grow and reach that as well. It will illustrate that your dreams and goals are possible. It brings out of the shadows the full picture of your future reality. Seeing that, witnessing that, is motivating. Make sure you surround yourself with people with work lives like the one you aspire to have.

3. Super connectors

Super connectors are people who are just super well connected. These can be friends, family, colleagues, or that

---

31. Anneke Jong, "You Can't Be What You Can't See: How to Get More Women in Tech," *Muse*, updated June 19, 2020, https://www.themuse.com/advice/you-cant-be-what-you-cant-see-how-to-get-more-women-in-tech.

guy from college who seems to know everyone. These are great people to have in your network because they always know someone you can talk to. You may be trying to research a new industry and have been reading a lot about it, but you have more questions. One of your super connectors probably knows someone you can talk to. Perhaps you want to learn more about the culture in a particular company and are trying to find someone to have an honest conversation with; ask one of your super connectors. Maybe you need expert advice on a subject. Yep, your super connectors have just the right person to talk to.

4. Mentors

Mentors can provide "a sounding board at critical points throughout your career," said Diane Domeyer Kock, senior vice president and managing director of managed creative solutions at staffing firm Robert Half. "They can provide guidance on career management you may not be able to get from other sources and an insider's perspective on the business, as well as make introductions to key industry contacts."[32] Your mentor relationships might be formal or informal, but they are people you deeply value who are usually at a different stage of growth than you are. They are available to you, will take your call when you have questions, and will provide insight and advice that you respect and admire. They might also champion you through

---

32. Matt D'Angelo, "How to Find a Mentor," *Business News Daily*, updated October 24, 2023, https://www.businessnewsdaily.com/6248-how-to-find-mentor.html.

introductions or recommendations that fast-track your access and opportunities.

Can you picture one person from your existing network for each category? Do you have a mentor, super connector, someone who has a work life you aspire to, and someone who is on a personal or professional growth path similar to yours?

Guidelines for Networking

Here are some guidelines to remember when building and nurturing your business relationships and growing your network.

The Most Underestimated Skill in Networking is Listening.

"To listen well is to figure out what's on someone's mind and demonstrate that you care enough to want to know," said Kate Murphy, journalist and author of the book *You're Not Listening*. "It's what we all crave: to be understood as a person with thoughts, emotions, and intentions that are unique and valuable and deserving of attention."[33]

When in conversation, instead of listening, too often we are planning what we will say next. When we leave those conversations, it is difficult to remember what we have learned

---

33. Kate Murphy, *You're Not Listening: What You're Missing and Why It Matters* (New York: Celadon Books, 2020).

from them because we were too focused on our contribution and not what the other person was saying. Listening helps to develop more robust and empathetic relationships with the people in our network. When we listen, we can learn how best to support the goals of the person we are networking with, what motivates them, and the challenges they face.

Listening also provides us with the insight to better understand the industry we are in or the ones we are interested in moving into. Chapter 15 discussed that an entrepreneurial mindset is critical to accessing the hidden job market. Our ability to understand the challenges an organization is facing, what they have and have not tried to solve the problem, and then offer a unique solution that includes hiring you to solve their problem requires exceptional listening skills.

An Engaged Network is Better Than a Large Network.

This bears repeating: it is better to have fifty people in your network who are engaged and responsive than five hundred who are not. Caring for and managing relationships with fifty people is more accessible than five hundred. Your community may have hundreds or thousands of people, but your network should be smaller. Focus on developing relationships with people you are interested in and those who are interested in you. Let go of managing relationships with those who are not.

17

Your Community is Not the Same Thing as Your Network.

You are connected to a vast world of other people through social media and other online communities. These platforms can be a wonderful place to build community, and even though they overlap, building community differs from building relationships.

Your community can be a powerful force of validation, support, insight, and feedback, especially when you have a large following or an established brand. For example, if you run a business or are a writer, they can help you refine your service offerings, help you research a topic, and become your customers. That's great! But your professional relationships require deeper conversations that benefit from a different kind of vulnerability than you can execute en masse on social media, or by going back and forth in the DMs.

It's Crucial to Understand Your Value.

As you build relationships, you each share in a mutual exchange of insight and expertise. You may be seeking different kinds of information and support from each other, but you're each providing value.

Change is humbling whether you are looking for a new job, starting a new business, or striving to get where you want instead of where you are. Even after twenty-plus years of bringing billion-dollar partners together and helping thousands of people get jobs, launch businesses, and improve their mental health, I still sometimes wonder about the value I bring into a room of entrepreneurs whose businesses are far greater than my own. I rarely feel that way in rooms with government officials, university leaders, and corporate muckety-mucks, but my goals are different now. They bump up against new vulnerabilities and require me to be in different rooms with different people—to show up, listen, and learn.

That vulnerability is okay—it's normal—but remember, we walk into any room, any conversation, as whole humans. Our value is far beyond simply the skills we may have or our work history. It includes our life experiences as colleagues, parents, and friends, as people who have gone through shit and come out on the other side. Allow that to be a part of your value, and show up.

The People in Your Network Are Not Your Personal Recruiters.

The people in your network are not your recruiters. It will be impossible to develop meaningful relationships if you only do it for the job hookup. People will see you coming a mile away and run in the other direction. Their job is not to find you a job, even though you will discover opportunities through your network. They will provide advice, support, and introductions that open doors to career alternatives that will change your life.

Main Takeaway

Don't complicate it. Life is short, so there is no point building relationships with people who don't share a mutual care and interest with you, or those you don't vibe with. When you start, it may feel like you are walking into the lunchroom in middle school hoping to find someone to sit with. It might feel awkward at first, but once you get the hang of it, you'll never again have to worry about where you will sit.

18

WHAT TO SAY WHEN NETWORKING

For me, words are a form of action, capable of influencing change. Their articulation represents a complete, lived experience.

—INGRID BENGIS

The two biggest challenges I hear people express about networking are "I don't know who to network with" and "I don't know what to say when doing it." We have discussed the power of the people around you, how to audit and design that group, and the four categories of people you need in your network. Now, let's dig deeper into *what to say* to them once you start talking to them.

Warm and Cold Connections

You already have warm connections and will be seeking out cold connections when building your network and developing your business relationships. **Warm** connections are the people you already know, and the people those connections introduce you to. **Cold** connections are the collection of people you don't know yet. Prioritizing warm connections is like skipping the line at your favorite hot spot or using a mobile order at your coffee shop; it reduces the time it takes to get to a meaningful conversation with the person you want to meet.

Remember, your network is just a collection of past, present, and future relationships. When trying to do new things, it is easy to think that we need all new skills, people, and stuff to excel. We forget all the people and expertise we already have that we can reengage to support our new activity.

So before focusing on cold connections, reconnect with those warm connections. This is the first step to engaging your network. Whether you have lost touch or not, you already know these people and have built a relationship based on shared interests. These individuals are the foundation of your network. As discussed in the previous chapter, run them through the "interest, care, and energy" rubric because there is no point in reconnecting with people you didn't vibe with or had no interest in, or who didn't really care about you.

Clients often tell me, "But Maryann, I've never had to network before, so I don't have a network." I remind them that yes, they do. They don't believe me until we brainstorm and map out their current network. They are surprised by how many people they know once they see it laid out before them. "Hell, I know a lot of people!" they say then.

"I told you!" I say.

The brainstorming exercise is simple:

1. To start, list the different **groups** of people you are connected to. For example, close friends, family, the CrossFit or yoga crew, faith communities, each online community you are a part of, the PTA, your old book club, your college alumni club, or other industry associations. List every group you can think of.
2. Next, write down all the **specific people** you can think of from each group. Write down how to contact them as well. For example, you can list Sally Smartypants, who you know from the mom group you were a part of when your kid was little. You usually contacted her via text, so you will write down "text, 555-123-4567." Or maybe you think of James, who is a former colleague. You follow each other on Instagram, so you will write down, "IG, @jamessomething."
3. Once you have **reached out** to each of these people, check them off the list and jot down the date and any relevant notes. This list will become part of your right-fit career growth strategy.

In the Resources section at the end of the book, I've provided you with a brainstorming worksheet to help you start mapping out your existing network.

The Anatomy of a Networking Call

Now that you've mapped out your network, it's time to get on a call and reconnect with everyone. Your networking call has four main elements: the **introduction/invitation**, the **conversation**, the **ask**, and the **follow-up/follow-through**. In the Script Guide in this book's Resources section, you will get real-world examples and scripts for each of these areas. In the meantime, let's unpack them.

1. The **introduction/invitation** is the warm or cold outreach you do to connect with people, ask them for a call, and make your first or next impression. This outreach doesn't need to be complicated; the simpler, the better. You could say, "Hi, Donna. I'm on a mission this year to do a better job of staying in touch. It's been a while, but I would love to catch up if you have time in the next two weeks. Are you up for a call?"

   Avoid lengthy explanations or updates in your message. The goal is to get them on a call to move the conversation from digital to analog. Ask one question; the example above is *Are you up for a call?* which is very direct and only requires a quick yes or no from the other person. Make it easy for them to say yes. If they say yes, respond with, "That's great! Please feel free to book directly via my calendar link. I'm looking forward to catching up." And include the calendar link. If they say no or don't respond, that's okay. Try not to take it personally. You have no idea what is going on for them; just be polite, thank them for letting you know, and move on to someone else.

2. The **conversation** is everything in between the introduction and the ask. This is when you get to know each other, talk about what you reached out to them to discuss, and ask any questions you have. Being prepared is essential; it improves the quality of your conversation and the relationship. If you are connected with them on social media, check out their latest posts to see if any life events have happened that might help the conversation or if you share an area of interest. Look at the kind of work they do: Does it raise any questions? Is it interesting or surprising? Does it make perfect sense, or is it a complete departure from when you both knew each other?

As a journalist and one of the best interviewers of all time, Terry Gross said, "I've always been really curious about things and slightly confused by the world, and I think someone who feels that way is in a good position to be the one asking questions."[34]

---

34. Marion Abrams, "What Is the Curiosity-Driven Interview Style?", *LinkedIn Pulse*, February 17, 2019, https://www.linkedin.com/pulse/what-il-curiosity-driven-interview-style-marion-abrams/.

Asking good questions is one of the hallmarks of a memorable and impactful conversation. So be curious, come prepared, listen, share, and see where it leads.

3. The **ask** happens at the end of the conversation. You must ask two fundamental questions at the end of every conversation. The first is, "How can I support you to reach your goals?" They may not have anything specific they need help with at this time, or they may, but always ask how *you* can help *them* before asking for help yourself.

Warm outreach is the most valuable currency in networking, so when it is time for the second question, your *ask*, ask for an introduction. For example, if you were discussing a specific work-related topic, you can say, "Is there anyone you can think of that I could talk to further regarding [insert topic]?" If they mention someone, respond with, "Would you feel comfortable making an introduction?" Or you can ask, "Do you know of anyone I could speak with who recently went through a career change?" Or you could say, "I'd love to connect with anyone working in [insert industry]; I'm interested in learning more about it to see if it might be a fit for whatever I do next." Always follow the ask by asking if they would be comfortable making an introduction.

On your networking call, do not ask if there are any job offerings or if they are hiring. It is not the time or place.

Plus, you can find that information on your own, so don't waste your ask on something Google can get you. If you know there is a job opportunity already, you have a strong relationship with the person, and you are transparent about wanting to hop on a call to ask about that specific opening, you can ask if they think you might be a good fit for the gig, or if they would be comfortable recommending you. This approach is only appropriate if the person knows you are reaching out to discuss the open job and they have welcomed the topic.

4. The **follow-up/follow-through** is everything that happens immediately after the conversation/ask. Unfortunately, most people forget or forgo this step, leaving a developing relationship languishing and unnurtured. During the follow-up, make sure you thank them for their time. If they introduce you to someone else, follow up to thank them for the intro, and let them know if you have a good call with that new person. If they give you some advice, follow up and tell them how helpful it was. If you say you will respond in two days, respond in two days. If you say you will send a link to an article that made you think of their post the other day, send it within twenty-four hours. Not only does your follow-up remind them of you, but it makes them feel valued and lets them know their support was helpful. I can't impress how impactful the follow-up and follow-through can be. Doing this will make you stand out and be remembered well beyond your peers.

Networking Ground Rules

Now that you know the anatomy of the networking call, and before you start reaching out, here are a couple of ground rules to remember.

Be Yourself

We are creating relationships here, so you are your best and most important asset in that process. Bring who you are to any conversation. You don't have to be perfect, know stuff you don't know, or hide the shit you do know. Be authentic, honest, and vulnerable where appropriate.

Be Clear and Transparent

Be clear and transparent in your communication. Don't schedule a call to talk about the time they spent working for company A and then jump on the call and start asking questions about company B. Don't misrepresent who you are or what you are looking for, and don't lie about your experience or lack thereof. If you are reconnecting after years of not talking, acknowledge how strange it is to reconnect. Be honest; it will break the ice faster. The more precise you are about your goals, the easier it is for people to help you. And if you still need to figure out what you want, say that. For example, if someone asks how they can support you, and you don't have an answer, say, "Thank you so much for asking; I'm not sure yet. Would it be okay to follow up with you later when I have a more specific answer?" That is a perfectly acceptable way to respond.

Come Prepared

Before any networking call, do your research and come prepared. Know who you are talking to, where they work, what that company does, what they post about, how the friend who introduced you knows them, etc. If you have invited them to a call, lead the conversation, ask good questions, and take notes on the conversation. Anticipate questions they might ask, and think about the answers ahead of time. They might ask you about what you do, what led you to start looking for another opportunity, why you wanted to talk to them, or your goal for the conversation. Make sure you have an answer to those questions and more.

Share Your Insight

You may have invited them to a call to learn from them, but you are developing a relationship, so it is essential for them to get to know you as well. Share your insight, experiences, and expertise. The better they know you, the easier it will be to remember and support you.

Respect Their Time (and Yours)

Respect their time and attention. If you set a call for 1:00 p.m., be on time and stick precisely to the time allotted. Make sure you are someplace free from distractions. If you are dealing with other people's interruptions, looking at your phone, or responding to notifications on your screen, it indicates a lack of interest and respect on your part. If you are taking notes during a video conversation, simply say, "I just wanted to let you know I may take a couple notes during our conversation, so if I am looking down, that is what I'm doing." This prepares them to know that you are listening and fully present during the time you are in conversation even if you glance away.

Make sure your video call setup looks professional, with good sound and lighting. Please, no calls while sitting in your bed, even when connecting with a past friend from your mom group. If you need to reschedule, apologize and immediately suggest another time. If someone stands you up, reach out once to reschedule, and if they do not respond or they stand you up again, move on. If they ghost you, move on; there are other people you can talk to. Your time is also valuable; save it for people who are interested and available—good advice for dating *and* networking.

Understand Your Impact

No conversation is one-sided; you have expertise and insight to provide to any networking conversation you are in. Along with knowing your value, which we discussed previously, ensure you understand your impact. Your impact is the results you deliver; it is the outcome of your skills, expertise, and service.

While your value is about you, your impact is about other people. It is about the effect your actions have on the things outside yourself.

Here are some examples:

- The results you have created for your company
- The way you make your employees, colleagues, or clients feel
- How you inspire your team members to do their best work
- How you have made the office more efficient and productive, saving your leaders valuable time and effort

Your impact can be measured through qualitative data, like any company performance metrics. It can also be measured through anecdotal evidence like peer stories, or reviews from clients and customers. Capture this impact so you can communicate it clearly to those you are speaking with.

Be Patient

Networking is a long game. It is about purposefully developing meaningful relationships to help support your goals, change your circumstances, and improve your opportunities. This takes time. You may feel desperate for a new job, but desperation is not a good energy to bring into your networking calls.

Don't Take Silence Personally

Don't take the "nos" or silences personally. People say no or don't respond for many reasons, and you most likely won't know what those reasons are. Do not take it personally or make it about you—it's not. They may have a personal or professional boundary that gets in the way. They may be swamped or on deadline and don't have the time. Something may be going on personally that you don't know about.

You have more than enough to think about; don't distract yourself by going down the rabbit hole of trying to figure out what is happening with someone else. Focus on you and your goals. Our brain tends to focus on the negative more than the positive. But do your best to interrupt that negativity by focusing on the future, your goals of finding that new right-fit opportunity, and, more importantly, how that new opportunity will make you feel and how it will change your life.

Main Takeaway

You already have a network; you just have to start talking to them. The initial outreach might feel awkward, but it will get easier as you get into it. Try and enjoy the opportunity to reconnect with past relationships, be yourself, and respect their time and attention. And remember, you are there to support them as much as you may hope they will support you.

19

SELF-PROMOTION AND YOUR CAREER STORY

I've said it before, and by gosh, I'll say it again—don't be afraid to toot your own horn.

—MELISSA STORM

I'm writing my story so that others might see fragments of themselves.

—LENA WAITHE

Making it through the career development journey is impossible without talking about yourself. You have to do it, as awkward or uncomfortable as it might be. "If you don't self-promote, your contributions will probably not be visible nor recognized, which will limit your ability to get a promotion, a raise, or important projects that will help you advance in your career," said Areen Shahbari, CEO of Shahbari Training and Consultancy and instructor at both Harvard and Stanford. "Many times, women think 'my boss should be able to know and recognize the value I bring.' That's not what happens in reality," Shahbari continued. "Managers in many cases are unable to quantify the specific value that you bring, and how much effort it took you to bring about a certain outcome, if you don't talk about it."[35]

In Chapter 8, we discussed at length why women struggle to advocate for themselves. In the workplace, women also face a double standard. When they do promote themselves, it can be viewed as out of line with feminine expectations and, therefore, off-putting. But if they don't talk about their accomplishments, their contribution becomes invisible. Women are often stuck between that proverbial rock and hard place, needing to be seen and acknowledged for the impact they create but burdened by unrealistic gendered expectations that make it difficult for them to talk about their impact. As is often the case, no matter the challenge, women will find a way to overcome it. Let's unpack how we can improve self-promotion and confidently communicate our impact to leaders, colleagues, and our overall network.

---

35. Pamela Reynolds, "Women Don't Self-Promote, but Maybe They Should," *Harvard Professional & Executive Development* (blog), July 11, 2022, https://professional.dce.harvard.edu/blog/women-dont-self-promote-but-maybe-they-should/.

Ways to Improve Self-Promotion

Craft Your Career Story

Your career story is the narrative of your professional life so far, with a nod toward where you would like to go in the future. It helps inform your business network, including colleagues, collaborators, mentors, recruiters, leaders, and hiring managers. It tells them

- who you are;
- the impact you deliver;
- why it matters to you; and
- the challenge you are interested in.

Skip listing job titles and company names; your career story is not a narrative of your résumé. It tells your professional story and carries the reader along your journey by tapping into the universal power of emotions. Your résumé provides facts and figures, and your career story brings those elements to life. It takes the reader on a journey that entertains and informs, painting a picture that transports them into your world. Taking the time to craft a compelling career story is a valuable asset in your career growth journey.

Storytelling helps us understand the experiences of others and closes the gap between assumption and reality. Your story humanizes the work you have done and shares why you are motivated to continue. It is an opportunity for connection. There might be something in your story that draws a leader to you: passion, drive, or a similar experience. Maybe it is the energy or humor with which you share your story that tells the audience about what kind of spark you will bring to a new team. Your career story is a dynamic compliment to all the other tools you have to communicate who you are and the impact you deliver.

To craft a compelling career story, you must not only understand the problems your skills are uniquely suited to solve and how you can solve them. You must also know where your passion comes from and where you want it to lead. Ask yourself: *Why do I do what I do? What do I like or love about it? What leads me to succeed or excel?* You may be driven by helping people, and got into your industry to do that. You may be ambitious and love the challenge of solving complex problems. You may be competitive and love the fire of beating the competition. Figure out what drives you, and share it in your story. Be honest, authentic, and memorable. People want to work with and help people they find interesting and capable—and, honestly, people who kick ass. Share who you are and what matters to you in the context of work.

Make it a habit to track your performance, whether you are required to or not. Once you finish a project, write down the quantitative and qualitative impacts. Experiment with what you track and how you track it; count everything. This data and information can be molded into your career story to support the narrative.

By shaping your story, you gain a better understanding of yourself and your professional path. You also create a persuasive narrative, an attraction tool that draws people toward you based on that story. By referring to your career story, you will stay focused and on track when you talk about yourself. It prepares you to speak and write confidently about your professional journey and answer any questions that may come up by reducing the stress of indecision and not knowing what to say or when. The more you tell your story, the more comfortable you will become at telling it; that comfort will build into confidence over time.

Write and Practice Your Power Statement

Your power statement tells people who you are and the impact you deliver, in one sentence. It is your quick and memorable answer to the dreaded "So, what do you do?" question. Drop it at all of your networking events to improve your conversations and develop better connections.

Create your one-sentence power statement based on the following formula:

"I am ___, and I do ___ for the benefit of ___, to achieve ___ [desired result]."

If the opportunity presents itself, also express why it matters to you.

Focus less on your previous job title and hard or soft skills and more on your experience, abilities, and accomplishments. You will have plenty of time to talk about (write about) those hard or soft skills in an interview or other networking conversations.

Here are some examples:

Example #1

Donna is a professor looking to transition out of academia into an opportunity to leverage her existing skills in teaching and training. She knows everything there is to know about learning and development. There might be some corporate software and frameworks she would need to learn, but she can put together a learning and development plan for any subject, and shape it to the needs of the learner with ease and creativity.

"I am Donna, an educator and learning and development expert who helps employees build the skills they need to further their goals and those of the organization they serve."

This is much more interesting than Donna saying, "I'm a teacher."

Example #2

Mary is looking for a team leader role in a corporate environment. She has spent a decade managing hundreds of people, events, and volunteers. She has an eye for detail, loves data, is mission-oriented, and is a team player. Mary used to say, "I'm a team leader at XYZ company." Now, she says the following:

"I'm Mary, and I help executive leaders build effective teams to solve complex problems, reduce inefficiencies, and reach company goals faster."

Which is more memorable?

Diversify How You Share Your Impact and Expertise

There are many opportunities to share your impact and expertise, elevate your profile, and promote your accomplishments without feeling like you are bragging. Once you understand the problem you solve and how your collection of skills is uniquely suited to solve it, it's time to share that information. Instead of sharing it to promote yourself, find ways to share it to serve others. Here are some examples:

- **Offer to do training** for other team leaders in your company, collaborating partners, or peer companies, focused on how you were able to reduce the number of meetings while expanding productivity, for example, and offer them steps for how they can do the same. In this case, you are sharing the impact you deliver while helping others increase their impact.
- **Speak at meetings**, industry conferences, or networking events, or participate in committees.

These don't have to be large events or meetings to be impactful; simply speaking up regularly or speaking at any size event will begin to raise your profile as an authority in your field. Let others know you are available to speak and looking for more visibility opportunities. Sometimes people don't think to ask, not because they are jerks but because their minds are on other things.

- **Create content** from your career story that you can adapt, expand, or condense and share on LinkedIn. Shape the content around helping people reach similar goals and the impact you have. Find ways to serve them through your posts instead of promoting your accomplishments.

Increasing your visibility is a great way of showcasing your impact by serving others instead of selling yourself. People will be able to see the value of your skills, the impact you deliver through the results at your company, and the impact of sharing your skills with others.

Make It a Team Effort

You are not alone. You may have coworkers and peers who feel overlooked or who struggle with promoting their own accomplishments. Whether through introductions, shoutouts in meetings, or extending offers to speak on panels or in meetings, praise your overlooked colleagues who are doing great work.

Thank those who do the same for you. We can all work together to make what may be invisible to others more visible to all.

Main Takeaway

You are going to have to promote yourself if you want to advance in your career. But there are many ways to highlight your accomplishments that align with your style and personality and don't feel like you are bragging. Explore some of those mentioned above, find the ones that work for you, and avoid the rest.

Section Three:
Career Momentum—What Gets in Your Way

20

THE INTROVERT/EXTROVERT NARRATIVE

I thrive on obstacles. If I'm told that it can't be done, then I push harder.

—ISSA RAE

We can have the best intentions, goals, and plans. Still, if we don't remove the barriers that get in the way of committing to our intentions, achieving our goals, and implementing our strategy, we make it unnecessarily harder on ourselves. Those barriers come in multiple forms: internal to external, physical to mental, financial to logistical, and more. They can be our self-sabotaging or self-limiting beliefs and behaviors. We can face resistance from the people closest to us. Or we may need more experience and knowledge—without which, we'd stay stuck. Anything can distract, dissuade, and divert us from taking the necessary actions to reach our goals.

In the next couple of chapters, let's dig into three of the most common barriers to finding your next right-fit career move.

The Introvert/Extrovert Narrative

I'm an introvert, so I suck at networking. You have to be an extrovert to be good at it.

The stories we tell ourselves create our understanding of who we are and how we fit in the world. We are born into a world of circumstances and expectations that pre-script those stories before we can write them for ourselves. So much of the narrative in our heads, and how we describe what we are or are not good at, comes from stories other people have told us, not the ones we have created for ourselves. It is easy to get attached to those stories. They form our identity, our sense of self, our relationships, and our societal roles. We often accept those stories without doing the work to understand or question them, but we have the power to change that.

Power is the capacity or ability to direct or influence the behavior of others or the course of events. Power is energy, force, and influence. The word "power" is essential in the context of our story because that story is the gateway to what we believe is possible. When we write our own story and stand in the power of that story, it allows us to influence our behavior and direct the events in our lives. If we give away that power—if we enable other people to tell us who we are and what we are good or bad at—we let someone else define us.

If you have internalized the story that introverts are "bad at networking" and you know you are an introvert or people have always told you you're an introvert, then you will think *you* are bad at networking. That's a terrible way to start. Whether you are an introvert, extrovert, or ambivert doesn't define your skill or success at networking. Anyone can be good or bad at it. The clarity of your goals and your commitment to developing engaged and supportive relationships is what matters. Your status as an introvert will shape *how* you network, but it has nothing to do with your ability to succeed.

Question the Story

Interrogating the stories you tell yourself, making sure they are yours, is an essential step toward achieving your career growth goals. To do this, we must first question what we know by asking ourselves, *How many of the stories I tell myself are told* to *me, and how many are created* by *me?*

In her bestselling book *Quiet*, author Susan Cain wrote the following:

> Introversion—along with its cousins sensitivity, seriousness, and shyness—is now a second-class personality trait, somewhere between a disappointment and a pathology. Introverts living in the Extrovert Ideal are like women in a man's world, discounted because of a trait that goes to the core of who they are. Extroversion is an enormously appealing personality style, but we've turned it into an oppressive standard to which most of us feel we must conform.[36]

We view networking as a playground for the extrovert, measuring our skill and ability against the outgoing, talkative, and confident behaviors we witness from the more social set. We assume that the extrovert model is the right way, the best way to build relationships, and therefore, we must conform. But that isn't true; the extrovert model is just one way to approach it, not the only way. Remember our previous conversation from earlier in the book about adding "for some" at the end of declarative statements? It applies here.

We live in a world defined by men—with long-held standards, expectations, and stories created by men. We have internalized them and live by them. Networking and the business orientation it captures have long been the purview of men because our business world is designed around their needs, behaviors, and style. But just because it has been done one way doesn't mean it is the only way.

---

36. Susan Cain, *Quiet: The Power of Introverts in a World That Can't Stop Talking* (New York: Crown Publishing Group, 2013).

Women have been developing relationships since the dawn of time, supporting each other, and excelling in a world that wasn't designed for them. We were creating informal communities of support long before psychiatrist Carl Jung dropped the terms *introvert* and *extrovert* into the early 1900s lexicon. Relationship-building is our strength, introvert or extrovert notwithstanding.

You don't have to network like anyone else; you get to decide what works best for you. Executive leaders Brenda F. Wensil and Kathryn Heath wrote for *Harvard Business Review* that finding informal opportunities to connect is essential:

> There's no need to get a lunch on the calendar, for instance, if you know the executive vice president is in line at Starbucks every morning at 7 AM... Arrive five minutes early to meetings and start a conversation. Walk to the train with someone you know is going your way.... Relationship building is never a one-size-fits-all proposition. Don't bother learning to play tennis if that's not your thing. Decide what you like—opera, ball games, wine tasting, trendy eateries—and invite a few colleagues along for fun. If you are an introvert, don't go it alone. Meet a few work friends and head to the company party with them. It's fine to work the room in pairs.[37]

---

37. Brenda F. Wensil and Kathryn Heath, "4 Ways Women Can Build Relationships When They Feel Excluded at Work," *Harvard Business Review*, July 27, 2018, https://hbr.org/2018/07/4-ways-women-can-build-relationships-when-they-feel-excluded-at-work.

You can reject the idea that introverts are disadvantaged when networking. You can ditch that false narrative, rewrite a new story, and build your networking strategy around your unique skills and circumstances. That is the power you hold.

Learn to Work with Your Strengths and Weaknesses

I used to describe myself as a closet introvert. I love people, but I don't necessarily love all of them in a room simultaneously. I prefer a meaningful conversation with a few, to working a room with the many. But I do it because I need to, because it makes my life and work better, and because I love people.

My career has required a lot of social engagement, community building, event creation and attendance, and partnership management. In the past, I would come home from a full day and evening of events, close the door, and stare at a wall to process and decompress. If the intro/extro conversation ever came up with peers and colleagues, no one would believe my introverted status.

When I was younger, that disbelief fed a sense of pressure to perform as an extrovert, to fit into the mold of someone in my visible, outgoing roles. Pretending to be something you are not is a bad idea, no matter how much pressure you feel. If you don't know who you are, it's worth finding out to avoid the charade.

As an introvert, when networking in person, pace yourself. Create a plan for what you want to accomplish and who you want to connect with, and permit yourself to leave when you have accomplished your goal, no matter how important the event is or what peer pressure you might be feeling. Doing more than you can or want to do doesn't make you better at networking; your strategy and intentionality do. Your ability to develop meaningful relationships in business and life will lead you to build a thriving career full of opportunity. None of that requires you to stay longer at events or talk to more people than you are prepared to.

Extroverts are often great at talking with people, are outgoing, and appear confident in social situations. That doesn't mean they are necessarily good at networking though. Networking isn't about being outgoing. Certainly, outgoing people who are comfortable talking to other people can be good at networking. But if they have no intent or strategy, are not good at developing relationships, don't know what to say, or say the wrong things, it isn't going to help them reach their goals.

One of the challenges that extroverts have is their lack of planning and organization. They talk to so many people that they often don't think more strategically about whom to talk to or follow up with consistently. Their confidence and comfort in social situations lead them to wing it. Therefore, they often build a wide but not very deep network.

My point is not to say that any personality type is better or worse at networking. The fact is that everyone comes to networking with their strengths and weaknesses. Everyone has room to grow, and everyone can succeed. Networking is a quality-over-quantity activity. It is about the quality of your conversations rather than the number of people you talk to or have in your network.

Check out the Resources section at the end of the book for more on how to network as an introvert.

Main Takeaway

You are the only one who can tell you who you are and what you are capable of. Question others who try. Your personality style is not what determines your ability to succeed at networking or developing the robust and engaged network that will help you find your next right-fit career opportunity; your strategy governs that.

21
TIME MANAGEMENT

You can have it all. Just not all at once.

—OPRAH WINFREY

Have you heard the story of the man who wasted his life taking drugs and playing Sudoku, and when he realized that he could do something meaningful, he worked hard and even got his time back? There isn't one because you can't get your time back.

—NEERAJ AGNIHOTRI

"I Don't Have Time to Network!"

Our time and attention are the most important commodities we have. We have a limited supply, but there is unlimited demand for it. That demand comes from everywhere, and everyone else thinks they have ownership over our time—our bosses, colleagues, kids, partners, parents, Mark Zuckerberg—and they do. They own our time when we let them.

Most conversations about improving time management center around how to be more efficient with the time we have in order to make room to do more stuff. This doesn't help; it just makes us busier and more burned out. Instead, the key is to reprioritize our time by understanding how we spend it in the first place and then reallocating that time to the activities that lead us to our life and career goals. Below are five ways to do just that.

1. Be Mindful of the Words You Use.

If you want to find that next right-fit career opportunity and build the kind of supportive and engaged network that will get you there, making time to network is essential. You don't need to *find* time for it or see if you *have* time for it; you are going to have to *make* time for it.

Linguist and author Amanda Montell says in her book *Cultish*, "A linguistic concept called the theory of performativity says that language does not simply describe or reflect who we are, it creates who we are."³⁸ The words we use matter. They shape how we will do the thing we are talking about. "With words, we breathe reality into being," Montell writes. Whether we are conscious of it or not, the words we choose indicate our commitment; they shape how we are going to do the thing we talk about and the actions we are or are not willing to take.

You have more control over how you spend your time than you use. When you say you don't *have* time, you give away the power of controlling your time to the person or thing that does. It could be a job, your kids, a partner, or a commitment that has usurped it. Making time for something indicates that you are willing to design your time around your priorities. You take control over how you use your time and direct it to the best of your ability. You can't control everything, but you can use the power you do have to shift your language, which will help get you started.

2. Tap Into Your Why.

Having a clear understanding of where your priorities lie makes it easier to set boundaries around your time when you feel yourself getting pulled in different directions. Roughly twenty years ago, the craziest thing happened: I popped out a kid and my entire understanding of time shifted. Pre-child, I thought I was busy and lamented not having enough time for everything. Once the little one came along, distinguishing between what I was willing

---

38. Amanda Montell, *Cultish: The Language of Fanaticism* (New York: Harper, 2021).

to make time for and what I wasn't became a breeze. My why was clarified by that bundle of poop and love, creating an ultrarefined filter.

I look back on the pre-child world and see my time differently. It took more work to determine the difference between not having *actual* time for something and not having the *desire* to spend my time on it. I spent a lot more time negotiating between what I *thought* I should care about and what I *did* care about. Understanding what matters to us is beneficial when directing our time and attention.

3. Let Data be Your Guide.

If we want different results, we have to change our current behaviors. And if we want more time to allocate, we need to know how we spend that time in the first place. Skip the assumption and let data be your guide.

We can *think* we know how we spend it, but we won't really know until we start tracking. By tracking your time, you will be able to identify clearly where your time is going, and to whom or what activity. The last time I did a time audit, I found I was spending an enormous amount of time watching movie trailers on YouTube as a way to detach at the end of the day, which was impacting my sleep, making the next day that much harder. I finally made the connection between scrolling and sleeping after I started tracking.

A time audit is an opportunity to reset your priorities, redistribute your workload, and empower others to take control of their own needs. It illuminates what time you use efficiently, what time you waste, and what time you give away. I have a time audit worksheet you can access in the Resources section at the end of this book.

4. Start Small.

You don't have to burn your whole life down to start taking your time back. It can happen incrementally. When we try to do too much all at once, it becomes overwhelming, making everything impossible. So skip the overwhelm and identify where to make minor adjustments instead.

If you want to reconnect with old relationships and start making new ones, look at your time audit and see where you can take back one hour once a week. Maybe you are binge-watching *Naked Attraction* on HBO Max every night, spending a lot of time preparing meals daily, or doing all the household shopping. You don't have to cut out everything all at once, but trim something. I know it's hard to look away, but maybe stick to just one episode of the absurdly naked British dating show. For shopping and meal prep, elicit some help from your family or friends.

Small actions turn into little wins, which cascade into progress over time. That progress will boost your confidence and propel you to keep taking action. Momentum begets more momentum. As entrepreneur and author Jim Rohn states, "Success is a few simple disciplines, practiced every day, while failure is simply a few errors in judgment, repeated every day."

5. Ask For Help.

We've talked about what makes asking for help difficult, but knowing that doesn't absolve us from doing it. It's time to get other people involved to help you take back your time. It can be hard to ask for help when you are usually the one helping everyone else, but you will get better at it the more you do it. Practice makes progress.

There are two important elements that will make asking for help easier and increase the quality of the help:

1) Don't wait to ask for help.
2) Be very specific about what you need help with.

Waiting too long and asking for help when you are in the middle of the chaos and feeling swamped will backfire on you. Also, just saying, "Can you help me?" is not enough for people to know what you need and how they can pitch in.

For example, if you want to cut down on the time you spend preparing meals, ask a friend to make a dish you love so you can freeze it and reheat the following week when you know you will be super busy. Or ask your partner if they can take on the responsibility of meal prep a couple of days a week. You can say, "Can you please be available from 6:00 p.m. to 7:00 p.m. to prepare meals on Monday and Wednesday?" And then negotiate from there as necessary. If they can't (or won't) help, move on and ask someone else.

People generally want to help. Those who care about you will do their best, and it will make them feel good to be part of your journey. And if the people closest to you don't want to help you or are unwilling, that tells you something about them too.

Main Takeaway

You don't find time; you make it. The key to making time is understanding where the time goes in the first place and reallocating it to your priorities. You can't do everything, and you shouldn't. Get help and focus your time on the actions that bring you joy and lead you to your career growth goals.

22

NEGATIVE SELF-TALK

The darkness, the loop of negative thoughts on repeat, clamors and interferes with the music I hear in my head.

—LADY GAGA

Why are you doing that?

You should just be grateful for what you have. Why do you always need more? Sometimes you're just too much. You have a great family. Why do you need to focus so much on your career?

Our self-judgment is a progress killer. It seeps in and zaps our confidence, motivation, and forward momentum. Often taking shape as our inner voice, it wields incredible power to support us or tear us down. Ultimately, it is more insidious than the voices outside our head because escaping can be more challenging. As previously discussed, we can demote anyone in our circles who does not support our goals, but it is harder to demote the conversation going on in our head.

Do you ever tire of people looking over your shoulder, telling you what to do, judging your choices, commenting on your every move? You must! You might have had a parent who did this, a teacher, a boss, or maybe a partner. You probably want to say, "Would you please just shut up already?!" It is awful to have someone constantly hounding you and reminding you about everything you are doing wrong. What's worse is when that person sounds like you.

But your inner voice is not you; the voice is a mirror of all the things others believe and feel and expect, and she is mostly full of shit. The key to managing your inner voice is similar to managing the external ones. If the input is constructive, positive, and motivating and it supports your goals, who you are, and the life you want to live, great. Listen to it, use it, welcome it. If your inner voice is overly critical, hostile, behaves like an asshole, and does not support your goals, who you are, and the life you want to live, it's time to shut her down. Here are four ways to do just that.

1. Recognize that she is not you.

Your inner voice represents a patchwork of good and bad influences. Most often, the voice you hear and the words delivered are not yours but someone else's. Maybe a parent, teacher, some other significant person in your life, a pastor, a friend—she is a tapestry of all the influences, past and present. Whether she is encouraging or a judgmental bitch, she is not you.

A cocktail of people, places, and experiences plays out to shape what we do, who we are, and how we think about ourselves. So take a step back and recognize that just because your inner voice is talking to you doesn't mean she represents how *you* feel about yourself.

2. Consider the source.

Before you absorb any positive or negative self-talk, consider the source. Now that you know the voice is not you, who is it? It might be the voice of your first boyfriend, the narcissist, judging you for actually prioritizing your feelings. It could be the voice of that great high school teacher who saw something in you when no one else did. It could be a grandparent who always gave you sage advice. It could be your inner child screaming out of intense fear.

Once you recognize the source, let that inform what you do with the feedback. You broke up with the selfish boyfriend for a reason, so there's no point in listening to his feedback. Grandma has always steered you right, so listen to what she has to say. See how that works?

3. Name her.

Give her a name. I've named my inner voice Charlie. Charlie tells me what she is thinking all the time. Sometimes it is useful; other times, she just spews my insecurities back at me, but I know her the moment she pops up.

Naming your inner voice is a psychological distancing tool, a way of stepping back from a situation to get some space, survey what is going on, and reflect on the best way to handle it without acting or responding too abruptly. It helps you gain perspective on the situation and generate a more appropriate response. By naming your inner voice, you slow or stop the momentum of the thought in your head and absorb less of what the voice is saying.

4. Have a conversation with your inner voice.

When Charlie has something to say, I have a conversation with her. I've tried listening to and ignoring her, but both make her louder. So now, I'll talk back. As with most conflicts, it is much better to deal with it in the moment than let it linger. Addressing your inner voice is the same way. The more you suppress her, the more she comes screaming back to bite you.

Depending on what Charlie says to me, I say, "I appreciate your opinion, but it is not useful to me today." When she is pushy, I say it out loud. If she gives me good advice, I say, "Thank you. That's good stuff. I'll use that." This provides my interaction with a beginning, middle, and end. It forces the conversation to be over and limits her power over me, helping to move through the thought more quickly without getting stuck in a thought loop.

Main Takeaway

Our inner voice can be an encouraging force, but when the judgy interloper version of her barges in, she makes everything we want to do and all we want to be much more difficult. Naming, taming, and understanding that she doesn't simply reflect your thoughts, but instead her words are an amalgam of many different influences positive and negative, is an important step toward controlling her influence.

23

HOW DO YOU KNOW YOU'RE MAKING PROGRESS?

And now, I'm just trying to change the world, one sequin at a time.

—LADY GAGA

One way to know you're making progress is to acquire what you want—when you get the promotion, receive the offer letter, or finally have the flexibility to pick up your kids after school regularly. Whatever it is that you are looking for, when you find yourself living the vision you had at the beginning of this adventure, you know you have made progress. Success is personal. You define what success looks and feels like. Other people's success is interesting, but it can be a distraction from what you are looking for. Progress is a journey, not a destination; it is a regular conversation you have with yourself.

Career development is a long game—the actions and habits you build will support you well into the future. The long game requires sustainability, which needs a sharp and strong mind and body. In that case, it is good to look at your progress in two ways: internal progress and external progress. **External progress** focuses on implementing your strategy, taking and tracking actions, and building the habits that will lead you to your next right-fit career. **Internal progress** focuses on caring for your mind and body while you work on that external progress.

External Progress

If you are networking your ass off but aren't sleeping, you are making good external progress but struggling internally. If you are eating well, finally limiting your alcohol intake like you have wanted to, and taking walks during the day, your internal game is strong. But if you still aren't doing the research necessary to see what opportunities are out there, your external game needs some work.

To maintain your external progress, take the time to track it. This helps you maintain pace, slowing you down or speeding you up based on where you are in the process. We can tell ourselves, *I have so much to do! I don't have time to write all this stuff down* or *I'm cranking! I don't want to stop to track; it'll kill the flow.* But if we don't

23

track, we will hit a wall, get lost, or feel doubt creep in when we look back at our strategy/action log and see nothing there.

I was recently diagnosed with an autoimmune disease and had to go on an elimination diet to figure out what foods were fighting my body the most. After cutting out almost everything I loved, I lost some weight. I signed up for a nutrition program to better understand how food was impacting my body, to learn how and what to track as well as maintain the results I had achieved. Horrifyingly, they required all participants to take half-naked pictures of our weekly progress. Uncharacteristic as that might be, I did what I was told, propped my phone on the stairs, and stepped back—three, two, one, snap. Even with all my bitching and moaning about it, at the end of the program, having a record of my before and after images was empowering.

Tracking is our external progress, self-monitor, motivator, and accountability partner. It is devoid of opinions and judgment. It simply presents us with day-to-day facts. If you want to save money, you must track your spending to know how the money is going out and where to cut back. As you review your accounts each month, you will be able to see whether you are making progress and adjust accordingly from there. So take the time and track.

Internal Progress

You are your most important asset in any life or career change. If you are not well in body, mind, and spirit, everything else suffers.

You know all those key performance indicators (KPIs) you've helped track throughout your corporate or professional career, love them or hate them, were helpful. It's time to define what your internal success measures are. What determines for you that you are making internal progress?

Start small. Pick one area you want to focus on. Maybe it is improving your sleep, drinking more water, or cutting out gluten. And I've got to tell you from personal experience, cutting out gluten wasn't as life destroying as I thought it would be. It could be committing to more physical exercise, getting out and walking every day, or actually going back to therapy, which you have been wanting to do. Whatever you choose, commit to it and track it. It will drastically improve your internal progress and help you reach your ultimate goal.

When you hit a little milestone, acknowledge, celebrate, or pat yourself on the back. Even better, give yourself a high five in the mirror. When interviewed by *Financial Post* about her book *The High 5 Habit*, here's what author and life coach Mel Robbins said:

> Get ready for me to blow your mind: Your subconscious doesn't physiologically know the difference between a

high-five from someone else and yourself. When you give yourself a high-five, even if you're thinking you're a piece of shit who doesn't deserve it, you get a hit of dopamine. It's neurologically impossible for your brain to beat itself up and accept a high-five at once. You will experience a slight energy surge, because your nervous system knows what a high-five is, and the gesture itself communicates for you. You are literally reprogramming your brain.[39]

Main Takeaway

Tracking and celebrating incremental action is how you know you are making progress. Whether it's better sleep and nutrition, increased exercise, or working your strategy and taking action, you will undoubtedly reach your goals. High fives, happy dances, pats on the back, nights out, coffee dates, taking a cruise to Madagascar, sleeping in, taking a day off, yelling "hell yes" in your house—however you choose to celebrate your wins, do it unapologetically.

---

39. Rosemary Counter, "Adopting This Weird Morning Habit Might Just Transform Your Life," *Financial Post*, October 12, 2021, https://financialpost.com/fp-work/giving-yourself-a-literal-high-five-in-the-mirror-every-morning-might-just-transform-your-life.

Here's What to Do Next

Damn, you are awesome! You have made it through from start to finish. You know a lot about me now, and I hope we can connect so I can learn a little bit about you. I look forward to you implementing the tactics, using the resources to determine what you do and don't want, create you career strategy, expand your network, and find your next right-fit career move.

The first step was picking up and reading this book. As you get started, here are four ways to keep the career growth momentum going.

Access All Your Free Resources

Remember all the "in the Resources section of the book" stuff. You can access all of those resources here! Visit **www.maryannlombardi.com/bookresources** to get access to all the resources mentioned throughout the book.

Find Your Next Right-Fit Career Move

If you found this book helpful, are tired of being stuck in your career, and are looking to expedite your progress to finding the next right-fit career move, I'd love to invite you to a call to learn more about you and your story. Visit **www.maryannlombardi.com/careergrowthcall** to schedule a call.

Hire Maryann to Speak

If you are looking for an impassioned motivational speaker for your conference, event, or mastermind, I'd love to bring it! Email maryann@maryannlombardi.com with "SPEAKING" in the subject line.

Connect on Social Media

Let's keep the conversation going. The journey doesn't end here. I'd love to connect with you on all social platforms. Let's have some fun!

Here's where you can find me on social media:

/maryannlombardi on LinkedIn
@maryannlombardi on YouTube
@iammaryannlombardi on Instagram

Acknowledgments

Thank you to my child. You are the light of my life. You are growing up to be the funny, heart-centered, brilliant, and beautiful human I aspire to be. Please don't be disappointed in me for not using your suggested book title. But I felt *A Snowflake, Zebra, and Fingerprint Walk into a Bar Even Though Only One of Them Has Legs* didn't accurately capture the content.

Thank you to Mary for being the most successful relationship I've ever had from picking someone up in a bar. You are the best bestie this girl could have and you mean the world to me. You also kick ass at book titles, thanks for helping me figure out this one.

Thank you to my parents for your patience, energy, attention, and the use of your house. Without all of those things, my story would be remarkably different.

Thank you to the many women who have shared their personal and professional stories with me over the years. They have provided me with not only insight into the world of work but also models for what vulnerability, strength, and resilience look like.

I need to give a shout-out to that Southwest Airlines ticket agent at Bradley International Airport in Hartford from Chapter 9. I wish I knew her name. Her calm control in the face of my chaos was the right gift at the right time. I've always wished I could have thanked her properly.

Thank you to the Big Idea to Bestseller Team: Jake Kelfer, Adrienne Dyer, Mikey Kershisnik, Tara Taylor, and so many more. You have made this process fun, and I've felt supported the entire way through.

Thank you, Sarah Linder, for doing all the behind-the-scenes business stuff you do to keep Find Your Fit afloat. Your energy, positivity, agility, and of-course-I-can-do-that attitude is a joy to engage with day in and day out.

Thank you to Jeremy for being the fun, adventurous, emotionally available man my own age (sorta) I didn't think existed. Your adventurous spirit, lack of motorcycle selfies, and love of good food, great conversation, and long naps makes my life better. Thank you to Cassie and Mary for your roles in making it happen.

Make a Lasting Impact in Real Time

Dear Reader,

Your perspective is incredibly important to me, and I would be grateful if you could take a moment to share your thoughts through a review. Whether you enjoyed the stories, discovered moments that resonated with you, or found the advice and insights helpful, your feedback is not only a source of encouragement but informs future writing topics and encourages others to pick up a copy. Thank you so much for considering this request, and I look forward to hearing your thoughts on my work.

About the Author

Maryann Lombardi, ambitious former executive turned business founder, is a bestselling author and single parent to the coolest young adult on the planet. As the founder of Find Your Fit, a career development company, she leverages her twenty-plus years of bringing together billion-dollar partners while working for governments, institutions, and brands to help women find jobs that support the lives they choose to live.

Throughout her career, Maryann has found herself miserable and burned out whenever her growth potential has stalled. She realized the most important thing wasn't the status of her positions but whether the work was challenging, had growth potential, and made her feel valued. She wanted to have an impact.

Her satisfaction (and the quality of her work) relied on the *fit*.

In her book, Maryann tells the story of her journey through divorce and family court, single-parenting, and career exploration that started in the cabaret clubs of New York City and led her to founding her company. She then guides you through her proven framework as you explore the life you want so that you can find your next right fit too.

Made in the USA
Middletown, DE
07 June 2024

55205997R00151